YOUR PERSONAL TRUTH

A Journey to Discover Your Truth, Become Your True Self, & Live Your Truth

I. C. ROBLEDO

www.RobledoThoughts.com

Table of Contents

Special Bonuses

For purchasing this book, I would like to give you *__three special bonuses:__*

1) An *exclusive eBook* that is not accessible to the public. It is called **Searching for Truth: 17 Questions to Separate Fact from Fiction**. This is an *actionable and practical guide* that will help you see more of the truth and stop falling for the lies that are all around us. With this book, you will gain a mental toolkit that will help you to perceive reality as it is. In order to make progress at anything, first you have to acknowledge reality.

2) *A list* of **I. C. Robledo's Top Book Recommendations**. Readers often ask me for ideas on what they should read next. This list contains about 300 of the most insightful books I have ever read. The titles are organized conveniently into these categories: Learning & Mastery, Psychology & Sociology, Personal Development, Business & Entrepreneurship, Biographies, History & Politics, Philosophy, Science & Health, and Literature.

3) *A guide* called **Step Up Your Learning: Free Tools to Learn Almost Anything.** If you have ever struggled to learn something, now you can discover free tools and resources to help you make rapid progress on your goals. It is essential that we learn something new every day, as this is one of the most critical skills that we possess.

You can collect these special bonuses by typing this into your web browser:

Mentalmax.net/EN

How to Read This Book

Through my experience writing many books, I've realized that most people struggle with applying what they read. We tend to read something, set it aside, and forget about the lessons. To help you make lasting progress in your life, I've included thought-provoking questions to reflect on at the end of each chapter. And I've also included activities to help you apply what you are learning.

To get the most value from this book, you should answer the questions and perform the activities. I put a great deal of time and attention into making sure that these would help you. They are just as important as the rest of the book.

As another tip, give yourself time to work through *Your Personal Truth*. Take the time that you need to make sure you understand the lessons. The process of growth and learning will take what it takes—if you are in too much of a rush, you may miss something important.

For those who prefer to read speedily, you may do that on your first read-through. You can then go back through the book more slowly, answer the questions, and do the activities on your second reading.

Regardless of how you choose to read, *you* will need to do the work to grow as a person. This book or any book can only be a tool to help you get there. But the real work comes from within.

An Introduction to Truth

"If you seek Truth, you will be alone forever.
You will not have the conversations you long
for. You will feel out of place in this world.
You will stand as a red spot against a pale
sky (And a beacon on the vast horizon)."

— Kapil Gupta

When I was 16 years old, my cousin Salvador asked me, "What do you want to get out of life?" I thought for a moment, and I said, "Truth. Truth is what I'm after."

I've been searching for the truth for quite a long time, and it has not been easy to find. The quote above by Kapil Gupta is the most precise quote I could find about what it means to seek Truth. If the passage scares you, that is okay. The truth can be scary. We must be brave nonetheless and pursue it wholeheartedly for ourselves. The fact that you are here reading this now demonstrates that you are ready.

Despite the ups and downs and twists and turns of my truth-seeking experience, I have learned great lessons along the way that could offer a road map to Your Personal Truth. This book will help unlock your journey and path that you must take to get to your truth. I will discuss my journey, but this is just to give you a hint as to what you may find on yours.

A core truth of mine is that we all have our own Truth. For many of us, this truth manifests as our own Tao—meaning a path, road, or way. Our truth becomes our way of life, which is why many of us can become so offended or upset if someone contradicts us. We take it personally because we have adopted certain ideas as being entirely accurate and irrefutable and as a part of ourselves. *When you refute my core truths, you are denying me and hurting me.* This is how we tend to feel, anyway.

Of course, some people will say that there is truth and falseness—and there is nothing in between. In theory, this seems reasonable. But in reality, there is so much that we do not know. There is no clear way to prove that something is true—we just collect more evidence to support an idea. But if one particular piece of data does not line up with the expectation, what you thought was true can be proven false. Often, our truths haven't been proven wrong *yet*.

Truth seems to depend on the time scale. Is a specific fact valid for a month, a year, decades, centuries, or millennia? Given enough time, the situation tends to change. What was true becomes false. Or what was false becomes true. For example, humans exist. You can look at yourself or those around you and see that this is obvious. But did humans exist 100 million years ago? No. Will they be here in another 100 million years? I would guess not, at least not in the same way that we exist today. The "Truth" that humans exist is limited by the period that we are looking at, which may be the case with countless other ideas.

If someone claims to know it all or have all the answers, this becomes problematic. In many cases, we may just hold different perspectives on an issue. Many of us will strive to find one single truth that will explain everything, but all we have in the end may be multiple points of view. You have your Truth or Tao, and I have mine.

Think of it. What types of perspectives do you tend to hold?

Keep in mind that mathematics offers a perspective. Someone's story or personal experience provides another view. Different authors on a topic provide different perspectives and approaches. But not all viewpoints are created equal. Some may have more support behind them than others. Still, they are different ways of viewing the world.

I see many truths in this world—many ways of seeing, believing, and perceiving. But when I was younger, I had this illusion that I must pursue one single truth. There was "the Truth," and that was all. It had this holy, noble feeling, but where is the evidence for a single truth? It would be simpler if there were just one truth, but in reality, there may not be a single fact in existence for which the whole world would be in agreement. Of course, a world of many truths sounds complicated and inelegant—we don't want to accept it, but this is a practical reality. I can have my truths, and you can have yours.

To elaborate, as a personal truth, one person may see the world as mostly happy. Others may see it as sad. The happy person smiles at everyone and sees that most people he comes across are also happy. The sad person goes around frowning at everyone and sees that most people he comes across are sad. The truths that we hold end up creating the world around us.

Our truths hold immense power. The ones we choose for ourselves tend to become our reality, the more that we believe in them. Everyone I know believes in money. And so, money holds tremendous power and is as valid as anything else. But if I find a remote society that doesn't use any currency, they will laugh at our paper money and tell us it is worthless. For my community, money is real and valuable. For another, it is as true as a child's imaginary friend.

I speak of truth here as depending on how much we believe in an idea or on our perspective, and this isn't the Truth we were brought up to understand. Truth for most of us is a matter of what is a fact and what is not. But I say that the facts depend on us, especially when dealing with our own lives, social dynamics, life choices, and values or beliefs.

When dealing with ideas personal to you, qualities unique to you, and your life perspective, you get to choose your truth. No one can decide some matters except for you.

Who will better know the truth of your life than You?

I am not saying that my truth is the sun exists, and perhaps someone else has an alternative belief. I say that maybe one person's truth is that we all need to love each other. Someone else's truth could be that we all need to love our closest family members and friends and not worry so much about the rest. Which one is true? It depends, as we will all have to select such truths for ourselves.

Laws, science, and mathematics can only answer the most direct and obvious cases of what is true and false. We must figure out our truth for all the gray areas or all the uncertainties of life. It just so happens that these uncertain parts of our lives can make up quite a large portion of life itself.

The real world will not provide us with an easy and direct path toward truth. You must decide that some things are true for you, and others are not. Suppose there is a lack of evidence for something that you used to believe. In that case, you can search for more evidence to see if there is another truth that you had perhaps not considered.

Some readers may be thinking that some things are a matter of belief, others are perspective, and others are truth. And that is fine. But my view is that there is a point where all of these things can fuse into one. I can get to a point where I understand something about myself so firmly that no one else on the planet could tell me otherwise. No one else could be a higher expert on who I am than me. And perhaps I could reach such a point with other things if I focus on them, learn about them, speak to experts, test out ideas for myself, and so on. There is a point where I can arrive at truths that others may refer to merely as beliefs. And I am okay with that.

I'm never going to figure out a truth that will convince the world. But if I can find the truth that convinces me, and I aspire to the highest standard of truth, then isn't that good enough? Doesn't that mean something?

Let's consider another example of what it means to search for a Personal Truth.

If I am interested in peace, and I learn all about peace, and I practice peace, then what will happen? Perhaps I get to a point where every single thought and action with me is peaceful. Then we can say that peace is my truth. In that case, someone comes to me and says I am a fool; there are wars, domestic abuses, gun violence, and so on all over the world. Then I tell him yes, that is the state of the world, but not the state of me. My state is peace, and peace is my truth. I have become the embodiment of peace.

But his life has become all about violence and frustration, and he smacks me in the face because he disagrees with me. When this happens, many people may question how peaceful they really are. But this situation would just be a test of how much I truly am at peace. I could redirect his attention to the birds singing and the kids laughing and tell him that there is peace waiting for him too. Or I could slap him back, but of course, that would shatter all of the peace I had created for myself.

If I spend my life struggling to find peace, and then I finally get there, and no one can take it from me, then my truth has led me to peace. This is Truth because it rises beyond the idea of perspective or belief. It becomes my life at that point.

Ultimately, this book is about asking yourself:

What matters in this life?

What is Your Personal Truth?

Facts that are well documented, such as the names of body parts, are not in question here. Look those up in an encyclopedia if you wish. But the truths that will guide your life, or keep you up at night, or lead you to your life's purpose are the ones that will matter the most to us in the end.

Your Personal Truths will be the ones that you work for, that are tested personally, that cost you a piece of yourself, but which give you so much more in the end. We will learn them through trials and tribulations. For example, when you thought you could go no more, and another obstacle presents itself. Yet, rather than slip and fall, you muster up some courage and strength and prove that you are better than you thought. This is when you learn new and profound truths that mean something.

Now, allow me to tell you how my truth journey began, as my cousin Salvador helped me embark on this path.

At just 16 years old, I realized that I needed to seek truth, but I had no idea how to do it. I had no road map, and I thought I did not have a guide. But my first guide was Salvador. One of the best thinking tools we all have is just in asking the right questions. I'm not sure how much longer it would have taken me to realize my life's purpose of seeking truth had he not asked me that straightforward question: "What do you want to get out of life?"

Now, I can see that many people in my life guided me along in finding my truth. Interestingly, the people who helped me never insisted that they had the one right way to show me. Usually, they showed me their perspective, way of thinking, or even the questions that kept them up at night. In some cases, I have seen people's truths in the way that they lived their lives. They are profoundly hardworking at something that matters to them. They are delighted and fulfilled with their lives, or they help everyone they can.

The truth is in everything that we do every day. To see it, we just have to sit back and open our eyes. Consider nature. Every day, nature is teaching us and showing us something. But we could ignorantly say that nature isn't telling us anything in words, in our natural language. The wind doesn't speak, and neither do the animals or plants. They don't express themselves in words, but perhaps they are communicating something to us if we just listen.

Sometimes I have had this Thought—*If I were lost in the wilderness, I would have to open my eyes to the truth of nature. I would have to observe where the animals are going and why. What are they eating and drinking, and where are they seeking shelter?* A mind stuck on needing to escape may panic. Instead, someone who can adopt the truth of nature may find a way to exist with it.

Just as nature often sends us signs, I like to imagine that there is some Truth out there sending me signs, and I just have to figure it all out. What about your Truth? Have you been receiving signals all your life and simply not paid enough attention? Maybe this book will help you to begin perceiving the signals of Truth that were already in your life all along.

As we begin, all I ask is that you open your mind, your eyes, and your life to Truth. I wish to show you the Way to your own Truth. That is my sole purpose here. I will be your guide.

KEY QUESTIONS

An Introduction to Truth

1. How would you define the word "Truth"?
2. What do you want to get out of life? (e.g., truth, knowledge, wisdom, happiness, love, success, or something else?)
3. Think of the critical perspectives you have been exposed to in your life (e.g., politics, religion, culture, geography, social groups, and so on). Are these giving you part of the truth or the whole truth?
4. When you focus on nature, what is the truth that you see there?
5. What is the most genuine part of you—your beliefs, thoughts, words, or actions?

TAKE ACTION TODAY

An Introduction to Truth

Action: **Think of someone in your life who is willing to ask uncomfortable questions.** For me, that was my cousin Salvador. He often asked questions that made me think more deeply about my goals and what I wanted to accomplish in this life.

Who is it that is willing to challenge you and even make you uncomfortable if needed? Who will help to open up your eyes to the truth and direct you toward meaningful growth in your life?

When you have this person in mind, give him or her a call. You can set up a meeting or send a text if you prefer. Mention a problem in your life or something that is holding you back. Ask if they would be willing to help you. Even if all this person does is listen, and you do the talking, this can still be helpful. Their silence will speak to you, and you will find some truth in that space.

Reason: The point of this activity is to find someone who you can confide in and who can help open up your eyes to the truth. The way to truth tends to present itself through a questioning mindset. When you discuss a problem, your confidant will likely ask many questions to understand what is happening. This process will help to shine a light on your truth.

Tip: Seek out a person who is *not* involved in the problem that you are dealing with. Also, be as truthful as you can in how you explain your situation. Do not try to convince this person that you are right and everyone else is wrong. Stick to the facts.

Your Fundamental Purpose is to Seek Out Your Personal Truth

> "Live your truth. Express your love. Share your enthusiasm. Take action towards your dreams. Walk your talk. Dance and sing to your music. Embrace your blessings. Make today worth remembering."
>
> — Steve Maraboli, *Unapologetically You*

To me, truth is about everything. Truth isn't just a matter of whether you tell the truth about something or lie about it. The truth runs deeper into our whole lives. Everything that we think, say, do, and feel is a part of our Personal Truth.

When you feel sad, if you do not discuss this with your spouse or your family, and if you wear a smile on your face all day, then in a sense, you are living a lie. To get at the truth, you would need to ask yourself: *Why am I feeling sad? Am I disappointed that something didn't go my way? Am I upset that someone mistreated me?* You have to explore what this feeling is, why you have it, and how it represents who you are to live your truth. A denial of your sadness or any other emotion you may have is a denial of who you are.

When you wish to go for a walk in the park, and there is nothing you would prefer to do, but your friends want to go shopping, then you may feel pressed into joining them. Perhaps if this happens once in a while, then it is not an issue. But if this happens regularly, where you would like to do something that none of your friends want to do, and you feel pressured into joining them—then you may feel the falseness invading your life. You may find yourself upset, doing things that you don't care about, being robbed of your time which you could have used to do something more entertaining or constructive. Understand that you live in falseness if you do not make changes to fix this.

When you value patience as an important quality but find yourself getting road rage, blowing up in anger, and yelling at other drivers, there is an incongruency. You believe that patience is an important quality to have, and we should be more understanding. Yet, you are not living up to this standard in your own life. When you defy your values and beliefs, then you are living in falseness. What is the truth? Is it okay to get impatient as long as there is something important you want to do? Or should you be patient under challenging circumstances? Usually, if a value is worth having, it is worth upholding even under difficult circumstances, isn't it?

The above examples are to show you that truth goes much deeper than our words. We can tell lies with our thoughts, beliefs, feelings, and actions. You may tell the truth with your words, but your tone of voice or body language could contradict them. Sarcasm is an example of this. Incongruencies such as this are forms of lying. Of course, often, the people around us will take note of this. When someone is phony, you get a sense for this, don't you?

Actually, it is not so easy to be a truthful being because to do so, your thoughts, beliefs, feelings, words, and actions would all need to align with no contradictions between them. This is difficult enough to do that most of us do not even try. Most of us focus on our words, and we may avoid telling big lies, or at least avoid telling them frequently.

However, it is a childish view of truth to only focus on the words we say. When we are children, we learn that we should say "please" and "thank you" to be polite. But if those are the only rules you follow, you have a relatively simplistic view of manners. Similarly, stating truthful words is the lowest level of being honest.

With truth being so important, we should meditate regularly or reflect on how true our thoughts and actions are. Think about it: if you are not truthful with yourself, you deny who you are. Essentially, if you are not truthful with yourself, then this means that you have gotten used to lying to yourself.

When we lie to ourselves, we will be lying to the people around us as well. We have to get away from those lies, as they help no one. Truth is the only path worth taking. It is more profound than we realize. It is our purpose.

For example, many of us may have thoughts like this at work: *I don't know the correct answer to the question I was asked, but I will say something that makes it sound like the question itself was foolish. That way, I can sound like I know what I'm doing.* A person with such thoughts may lie to himself regularly, telling himself that he is the best and most knowledgeable worker at his job. In reality, he often struggles and blames his ignorance on everyone else.

And this brings us to an interesting point. When we lie to ourselves, we are often doing this to protect ourselves from the truth. Yet, much of the time, deep down, we already know the truth. We have simply hidden this from ourselves so that we could be in enthusiastic and positive spirits. But that positivity is just a facade if it is due to a lie.

This protecting of ourselves is unnecessary. We treat ourselves as if we are so fragile that we cannot handle a simple truth, but this is not the case. In my life, I have seen that we are all much stronger than we think we are. We can handle much more of the truth than we think we can. It can hurt deeply at the moment, but then we learn to move on. This is better than living a lie.

In the past, when a truth about myself came to light that was uncomfortable, I was often unhappy to realize this truth at the moment—but in time, I was grateful for it, as I was able to improve quickly when I realized what the problem was.

For example, I once had a manager call me aside and tell me that I was not a team player. She was correct that I was not contributing to the team's objectives in our meetings. I did focus on my work, and I made sure to finish all of my tasks, but I was like a sack of potatoes during meetings, zoned out. At first, I was upset that the manager had bothered me about this. But then I realized that what she had said was true, and I needed to do more. It wasn't fair that everyone else contributed and worked on our objectives, and I was merely on the sidelines. Meetings were an essential part of my job—I just had to remember that and take them seriously.

It can be difficult and painful to acknowledge these truths. Still, they generally provide us with a path toward growth and betterment. Resist the urge to hide from these painful truths. Do not get trapped into feeling upset about something that happened. Instead, take what happened, see it for what it is, and plan to do better.

The reality is that when we hide the truth from ourselves, usually we are hiding from ourselves. There are parts of us that we do not like, and so we pretend they do not exist. This means we create fantasy worlds in our minds around what is happening. We trick ourselves into thinking that things are fine, even if they are not. In time, problems build up more and more, and we continue to lie to ourselves, acting as if there are no issues. One day, these problems blow up in our faces, and something happens that cannot be undone—we lose a job, relationship, or suffer some horrible tragedy.

When telling lies, it is tempting to say another and another until we end up believing our own lies. Eventually, our lies cannot overlap with the real world. We push things too far, and they crumble to pieces in front of us. The lies collapse, and potentially our lives as well.

Seeking out your truth is ultimately about figuring everything out. If you are the type of person who has a response or solution to everything, then perhaps you already have a good sense of your personal truth. Nonetheless, there is always something new to learn.

Your truth may be that your family comes first, and you will do anything and everything that you need to do to make sure they are safe and well taken care of.

Someone else's truth may be that his life mission is to be a paramedic helping people who suffer all kinds of injuries.

Another person's truth may be that all she wants to do in life is be happy. She doesn't want to worry about all the minor problems—she wants to pursue happiness and help her loved ones do this.

Of course, anyone could have multiple truths in their lives. For instance, my family, work, and quest to learn and understand many different domains are all parts of my truth.

However, there is a truth that rises above the rest, which is the focus of this book:

We are here to pursue our truth and to live it out.

For some people, this may be easy. We all know someone who had everything figured out since he was a child. He knew what he wanted to do from a young age. He worked hard at it and ended up becoming quite successful. However, for most of us, life is not quite that simple. In due fairness, even for the person whose life seems straightforward, they will likely face many challenges as well.

If you have ever been pained to choose a college major, career, or relationship, then you have probably struggled with pursuing your truth. This struggle is part of the process. It is your induction into finding your personal truth.

I want to help you find your truth because it is a core concept that influences *every* part of our lives. This is such a broad idea that some people may think it is not helpful to focus on Truth as a general idea. Instead, they may believe that we should focus on finding purpose, telling the truth, or learning about ourselves. But I would say that it's worth trying to go all the way, to discover as much of our truth as we can. In doing this, all the significant parts of our lives will come together into one unified whole.

We must strive to live out our truth because we have so many different sides of ourselves that can conflict if we allow it to happen. Instead, we need to strive for personal harmony. This harmony is our truth. When all parts of yourself are working together as a harmonious self, then you have found your truth.

Truth, essentially, is about becoming our actual selves. We are born and taken care of by parents who raise us according to who they think we should be. Still, after a certain point, it becomes our task to determine who we actually are.

Is your truth the same as your parents and the people who you grew up with? Is part of it the same? Is your truth entirely your own and not overlapping with theirs at all? Either way is fine, but the key is to search for your truth. This is the journey you were meant to go on.

Early in life, you may have been living out your mother's or father's truth or an older sibling's truth, but at some point, you have to ask yourself: "What is my truth?" Whose life am I going to live—mine or someone else's? "Whose failures am I going to live out—my own, or someone else's?" When you live out someone else's life, you will live to experience failures that were not your own. This may be the worst failure of all.

One of the greatest truths of all is that we are here to find our truth. Doing so means becoming who we were meant to be and accomplishing what we were supposed to accomplish. The alternative is to wander, to feel lost, to be uncertain about who you are and what your purpose is. This is a part of life too, but hopefully, we can learn to strive for our truth efficiently and minimize the time we wander and feel lost.

Let's consider for a moment—what happens if you simply don't seek out your truth, and you ignore it?

Unfortunately, those who don't seek out their truth may end up living out someone else's life. They may end up lying to themselves about who they are and fail to understand themselves fully. Such persons may not live up to their full potential. They will have inner conflicts, pulling themselves in different directions. They may easily trust what someone else claims to be the truth, as they have failed to develop their core or inner source of truth.

At the end of their lives, they may come to see that their whole life was never their own. It was all a lie, in a sense. This is a tragedy to be avoided.

Contrary to what it seems, Truth isn't only for those willing to search for it. It's also for those who are ready to peel back the falseness and see what is there, which is their true selves.

At this time, society is not built to help you find your truth. Suppose you have caring parents or an excellent educational system. In that case, you may be lucky to find some people who will help guide you toward your truth. But more often than not, the people and systems around us want to teach us their version of the truth. And they do not want to hear anything that conflicts with it.

Understand that our truth ends up becoming a part of ourselves. If someone challenges your deepest thoughts, you will naturally feel threatened. This is something we must learn to overcome. You should feel safe to challenge someone else's version of the truth, and others should feel safe to challenge yours. This is how we grow, adapt, and learn. The challenges are a good thing, not something to be avoided.

Before challenging someone's truth, however, we have to perceive it for all that it is. A way to do this is to practice perceiving *Fields of Truth*. For

17

example, when I see someone, or if I see their living space or workspace, I can sense a field of energy that is their truth. Here are some qualities I may notice: orderliness, cleanliness, photos or objects that indicate specific values, and the ability to think critically. These and other attributes will give you clues as to a person's Truth.

Attune yourself to other people's Fields of Truth. Allow your mind to empty itself occasionally so that you may see how others are seeing the world. Many of us get stuck on thinking: *What am I going to say next?* Or, *What will I do next?* Forget those things, and instead focus on what is around you, and open yourself up to that Truth.

If you do this, you will open yourself to other people's ways of seeing and perceiving. Then in time, you will come closer to your own Truth.

KEY QUESTIONS

Your Fundamental Purpose is to Seek
Out Your Personal Truth

1. Are your thoughts or beliefs in conflict with your actions?
2. What are some thoughts you often have that serve to protect yourself from an uncomfortable or inconvenient truth?
3. Has anyone tried to convince you of their truth recently? Were you open to this or not?
4. What are the most critical three parts of your life? (e.g., specific values, priorities, or goals)
5. What is an irrefutable truth in your life? This may be about yourself or life in general.

TAKE ACTION TODAY

Your Fundamental Purpose is to Seek
Out Your Personal Truth

Action: **Write down a Truth that you hold inside of you which has not been heard in your life.** Perhaps you have a dream, but the people you care about do not want to listen. Maybe something happened to you, but most people think you are exaggerating or they simply don't believe you. Otherwise, perhaps you are worn down daily because you feel you must live your life in a particular way, even though doing so goes against your will.

If it helps, **think of a time when your feelings were hurt.** Sometimes, this happens because an essential person in your life is not listening to your version of the truth. Or maybe someone has not accepted you for who you are. Is there a part of you that you have struggled to express?

Reason: To go on the path of truth, it helps to think of one that was denied in your life. When you acknowledge something that has not been adequately heard or expressed, this will help you begin Your Personal Truth Journey.

Tip: No one needs to read this. You can write down your thoughts and then throw them away right after if you want. But writing is a powerful activity that can help us articulate truths that we have been hiding from.

No One Can Give You Truth—You Must Seek It for Yourself

"Believe those who are seeking the truth. Doubt those who find it."

— André Gide

No one can give you Truth. This is for many reasons, but a key one is that you are the only person with your perspective in life. Imagine the goals of an insect. It needs to find food and to avoid getting eaten or killed by bigger creatures. These are the fundamental truths of its life.

But you are not an insect. You are a human being in a unique situation and context. So the truths most important to your life will be different from an insect or any other human being.

I enjoy reading books to learn other people's truths, but those truths are usually written by someone in a completely different context, who grew up differently, and who had different struggles, opportunities, and ways of viewing the world. As much as I may enjoy a book, I always keep in mind that those are someone else's truths. I have to figure out my way.

Even if someone's truths make a lot of sense to me, I will process them in my way and come to my understanding of them. It isn't helpful for me to read something and then copy and paste their ideas into my mind. I believe that ideas were meant to grow and evolve.

Our lives and worlds are constantly changing and adapting. So the ideas that we view as truths must also grow and change and adapt to our personal circumstances.

No one can give you Truth. *Think about this:* If I give you the truth and you accept it from me because I am smarter, wiser, I have read more books and am more educated, or for any such reason, then you are accepting something as truth without having thought about it or figured it out for yourself.

I might as well have fed you lies because sooner or later, someone will, and if you are not thinking critically, you will eat it up.

Understand that the truth does not come easily. In reality, you must figure it out for yourself. The uncomfortable truth about truth is that it isn't easy to find. No one will give it to you. And even if they do, you should go through the hard work of figuring out how much of it truly applies to your situation.

You have to get used to asking yourself questions such as:

- Is this true?
- Is this NOT true?
- How would I know the difference?
- Is someone trying to get me to believe something because it benefits them?
- How can I trust whether this person or source has the whole truth?
- Does this make sense? (e.g., using logic, common sense, wisdom, intuition, or reason)

As human beings, we trust too quickly. Every day I make a short drive to drop my wife off at work. On the way, I usually see a couple of people crossing the street while looking down at their phones. Glancing at a sign that says "walk," then crossing the street while distracted with a phone is like getting all of your information from one source and believing it without question. When you see the "walk" sign, you are only getting your information from one perspective. Another perspective would be to look around before you cross.

Perhaps there is a drunk driver who doesn't care what the truth is. He had too many drinks, and all the lights look green to him as he struggles to stay conscious. Or perhaps a few teenagers took a car for a joy ride, and they don't even have their driver's licenses. If that were the case, you would want to be more alert, not distracted.

The "walk" sign tells you that society generally agrees you should be able to cross safely, but this is no guarantee in the end.

What are the "walk" signs that you trust to tell you the truth in your day-to-day life? Is it the news? Your closest friends? People who have degrees or titles?

Keep in mind that there is no single, easy path toward truth. Ultimately, every situation can be seen from different points of view. Open your mind to seeing more perspectives, and this may help you to find your truth.

As an example of why it helps to open your mind and see things from more points of view, consider this. If you go to the library and learn about black holes in an encyclopedia, the information may be wrong because it is out of date. Suppose you read about the same ideas in Wikipedia. In that case, the information may be incorrect because, as a joke, someone filled the page with errors. In essence, every source you learn from could have some mistake or falseness in it. Just the same, any single point of view may fail to provide you with the whole truth.

When you learn from a wide spread of sources, however, you can smooth out the errors. You can see that some facts are stable, and they are consistent in how they are referenced. Or you may notice that other "facts" are unstable, and they are often reported on inconsistently, or where scientists and other experts tend to disagree with each other.

In general, we should be willing to absorb the truth of scientists and experts if they mostly agree on something. And, of course, if it makes sense, it is logical and reasonable. But what if they don't agree, or what if the information is rational? In such cases, there is room for you to come up with your version of the truth. This doesn't mean that you just make up a convenient story that suits you. Instead, it means that you use your mental resources to develop an understanding, likely by considering some expert information and analyses.

What we often forget is that there are errors or falseness in everyone's version of the truth. No one holds the perfect version of the truth all on their own. *Consider this:* have you ever noticed how easy it is to spot the flaws in how others think, but it's not so easy to see this in ourselves? We tend to believe that our way of thinking is perfect and truthful because we fail to identify the flaws in our mindset.

Something else to consider is that just because the people around you tend to hold similar views does not make them correct. All it means is that they have generally had the same experiences and spent time with people who thought and believed in the same ways.

There is a quote I recall from memory, and unfortunately, I do not know the source. Here is my recreation of it:

"How is it that a person's soul mate almost always ends up being someone who lives no more than 50 miles away? Isn't it amazing that out of all the people on the planet, this was the person who was meant to be our one true love, and they happened to live so close?"

You may have heard of something like that in the past. Many of us understand the idea when it comes to relationships—we all want to think we found the one true love of our lives. Still, rationally, it's hard to convince ourselves how we just happened to have the luck of finding this person close to where we grew up or lived. Perhaps your true soulmate was born in another country and spoke another language. Maybe they were even born in another century.

Yet when it comes to understanding truth, we often fail to see this same pattern. The chances are that where you grew up, many people tended to have a particular way of viewing the world. They had their version of the truth, and by growing up around them, you absorbed that version of the truth as your own. But out of anywhere you could have been born, how lucky must it be that you happened to grow up in the one place that understood the absolute truth? Instead, isn't it much more likely that you were raised with a particular perspective, which perhaps was a *version* of the truth?

Pay attention to my language here. I do not believe life is so simple. We are not always dealing with absolute truth and absolute falseness. Often, we have different *versions* of the truth or different *degrees* of the truth.

For example, consider the famous Indian parable (translated by John Godfrey Saxe) about six blind men presented with an elephant. But never having seen one, they do not know what it is. So they begin to feel it in different places.

> *"Hey, the elephant is a pillar," said the first man who touched his leg.*
> *"Oh, no! It is like a rope," said the second man who touched the tail.*
> *"Oh, no! It is like a thick branch of a tree," said the third man who touched the trunk of the elephant.*
> *"It is like a big hand fan," said the fourth man who touched the ear of the elephant.*
> *"It is like a huge wall," said the fifth man who touched the belly of the elephant.*
> *"It is like a solid pipe," Said the sixth man who touched the tusk of the elephant.*

The men began to argue about the elephant when a wise man passed and told them that they were all correct. It was all one creature, and they had all felt a different part of it. The blind men understood then and stopped arguing.

Truth may be like an elephant. We all get glimpses of something that we all see parts of, yet we think we see the whole truth. We have become convinced that our Tao or Way of Truth is THE way, which is quite unlikely to be the case. Perhaps you are right about your truth, for your own life, but if you assume that this makes other people wrong, you may be mistaken. There may just be different versions of the truth that we are all seeing, as there are different parts of the elephant that the blind men can experience.

Now you can see that for any truth given to you, it is not actually given because you must think it through. You must process it and consider whether that truth deserves to be a part of your personal truth. Consider if someone's perspective can be adapted to your circumstance. Can you apply it or somehow make it relevant to your life? Does that truth offer something useful for you, or not? Is it best forgotten, or should you keep it in mind in case you can use it later, even if it seems irrelevant at the moment?

If you meet someone who wants to give you "the truth," and he is adamant that you must listen to him, then this is a situation where you have reason to be skeptical. Why is this person so persistent in wanting you to see their version of the truth? Perhaps they want to help you, or maybe they want you to believe what they do because it will help them achieve their goals. It is also possible that they may have been given something they thought was the truth. They never questioned it, and now they believe it makes sense to try to convince you of it.

We must question the truth, digest it, process it, and get a feel for it. The truth is not something to idly sit by at a screen and take in, absorbing it. You choose—which parts are worth focusing on, which ones should be set aside to consider more deeply, and which should be rejected, as they simply do not align with your true self.

Perhaps most of the people around you agree on certain truths. But even for those truths that seem obvious, it helps to think them through. You may develop improvements to versions of the truth that others have simply assumed to be the case. You may find that you don't fully believe some widely accepted ideas. Or you may find that some of them do not make sense to you or that they create injustices. They may even be based on flawed reasoning or come from a leader who has not been adequately tested or questioned.

At its heart, getting to the truth is about actually thinking. We believe we are learning to think for much of our lives, but perhaps we were learning *not* to think. When faced with one type of problem, we were learning that you solve it by following a specific set of steps. We were learning that when an authority tells us something, we do it without questioning. We were learning that there was only one way to perceive. Possibly, some of the fundamental things we learned were wrong. Maybe if we had been taught to question more, we would have learned to think more deeply and to discover our path toward our truth.

The reality is that most of us tended to follow the truths that were conveniently laid out for us. As I said before, what are the odds that the particular beliefs of the people around you just happened to be the one complete and accurate truth? Maybe it is just a part of the whole picture.

The reality is that no one will give you the truth. You will need to seek it out for yourself. Then you can learn to think for yourself and ultimately decide what is legitimate and not for yourself.

Of course, this is not easy to do, but this is the path toward your truth.

Other paths often just lead to blind acceptance of someone else's version of the truth.

I encourage opening your mind to different perspectives and possibilities. Think for yourself rather than waiting for someone else to do it for you. Also, ask difficult questions and do not settle on solutions just because they are convenient. Doing so will help you to understand what is true for you. The most important thing in life is to discover Your Personal Truth

KEY QUESTIONS

No One Can Give You Truth—You Must Seek It for Yourself

1. How often do you ask yourself challenging questions about yourself and your life's experiences? Could you benefit from doing this more?
2. Did you ever expect someone to give you Truth? Why do you think that was? How did it turn out?
3. Do you often provide your version of the truth to people in your life? What makes you feel so strongly?
4. Is there a life perspective that you assumed to be fully accurate—then later found that you disagreed with?
5. Did someone ever share a truth with you, and you were grateful for their eye-opening perspective?

Action: **Come up with your definition of an important concept in your life.** I would challenge you to explore some concepts that are viewed as fundamentally important by many but where people often disagree with what they mean. Keep in mind that their disagreement implies that there are different perspectives or truths about these ideas.

For example, *consider what these words mean to you:*

Love, happiness, family, friendship, good, bad, knowledge, wisdom, trust, truth, pain, grief, money, and honor.

Pick one that is the most important to you, or that is currently most relevant to your life.

If you don't see a word that appeals to you, come up with your own. When you are ready, write down your definition of it. It's vital that you *not* look it up in a dictionary. I recommend coming up with your meaning of the word.

Reason: When it comes to important ideas, accepting someone else's definition is just accepting their truth. In our youth, we accept the perspectives around us as truth, absorbing them. Even as we grow older, many of us will assume that these truths that happen to surround us are the absolute truth. Still, the challenge of our lives is to understand that they are just perspectives and that it is up to us to pursue our truth. As adults, one way to begin on this path is to define words and ideas for ourselves.

Tip: Don't settle for a short one-sentence definition. If something is critical to you, work on defining the boundaries of what the word means. For example, with the word "Love," at what point is intending to love not good enough? At what point is a loving gesture meaningless if there is not a track record of loving actions? When are loving words not enough? Where is the boundary between loving and not loving? How do you know when you see it? How do you fall in love, and how do you fall out of love? Are there some unbreakable bonds of love? And why?

After you have written your detailed definition of this concept, you may look up the word in the dictionary or look up how other people have defined this word online. How does your definition compare to theirs?

The Truth is Elusive and We Must Redirect Ourselves Back Toward It

> "Truth is, in fact, an elusive concept. It depends almost entirely on where you are standing at the time. It is a human instinct to confuse belief with truth."
>
> — Gwen Ifill

You may have gotten the idea from what you have read in earlier chapters that the truth is elusive. That's because it is.

Eventually, you will find clarity on your truth journey, but it tends to escape us in the early stages. Have you ever found yourself frustrated in wanting the truth, yet there being no clear path to get there? Of course, just because you want it doesn't make it conveniently pop up in front of you.

Seeking truth can be frustrating, and I understand that some people may find it easier to forget about it. They may just want to live their lives comfortably and serenely and not have to worry about the truth. Or they may find it easier to assume that everything is precisely as it seems and entirely truthful. But such ideas can turn into denial. Wanting things to be true does not make them so.

I am on a quest for truth. And I hope you will join me.

Some of the greatest joys I have found were in figuring things out for myself. In 2020, I began writing down my Truths for the world to see at www. RobledoThoughts.com—you are welcome to visit. I do not want anyone to accept my truths blindly—instead, I want you to use my writings to help figure out everything on your own.

Just remember that at the beginning of your Truth Journey, the truth is elusive.

Part of the reason for this is that many people and big ideas in our lives can be contradictory. Who is right? Everyone insists that they are correct, but often the opinions of different groups conflict. Everyone can't be right. So who should you trust?

What truths have the key people in your life been pointing you toward?

Consider your parents or the adults who raised you. Based on how they live their lives, you have probably learned tremendous amounts from them. Sometimes, you may have not even realized that you were absorbing ideas and habits from your parents. For example, when your Mom gets anxious, how does she react? How about your Dad? Do you have a similar reaction as one of them? If you do, it's easy to assume that it is genetic, but quite likely, this is something you absorbed in your upbringing. You saw the patterns that your parents went through every day, and some of those became your own. It became the default way of living your life.

Perhaps even, it became your truth.

Consider this: When you were growing up, did your parents respect or admire people of certain professions? Did they like their jobs? Did they value making money or following their passion? Did your career end up reflecting their wishes, or did you go on a different path?

Did you adopt their truths or discover your own? Or something in between?

Our parents have a tremendous influence on us. I know many young people do not want to believe this or even refuse to believe it. But when you spend so much time with your parents, their actions will impact you.

Many other forces influence us beyond our parents. What country did you grow up in? People in different countries tend to make different assumptions, believe different things, and even perceive differently. What do you think culture is? Ultimately, it is an expression of a country's truth. What most people in the country believe is truth will decide how that country's people will behave. Suppose you have adopted your country's way of perceiving reality. In that case, you will identify with the dominant culture—if not, then you may identify more with a subculture or perhaps just walk your unique path.

What about your friends? What do they think, believe, and feel? Has that influenced what you believe to be true? Often, our peers or friends will have different viewpoints than our parents or elders. They will have separate interests as well. As with all groups, there is a vast amount of variation. Some friends may encourage us to become apathetic and waste time, insisting that nothing matters. Others may be ambitious and work hard, following their parents' wishes. Others may find it essential to make time for work and have fun—they may just accept it as a part of life that you work even if you don't like it so that you can make money to have fun. Perhaps your friends have different beliefs or ways of thinking and seeing, and that is fine.

The point is that you will be exposed to their truths every time you see them. These friends will not necessarily tell you their Tao or their way of being and seeing, but they will be living them out through their actions. One friend may unexpectedly stop by your house, requesting that you accompany him to a concert. He is telling you with his actions that everyone should always be ready to start an adventure—life is about spontaneity. Another friend says he is busy studying or going to church when you call him—his life is more structured, about responsibility, and planned. There is no right or wrong way. But in being exposed to different people's truths, you will start to get a feeling. What feels right to you? What is your truth?

We can even go deeper. Perhaps a school (or club, or event) you attended was known for being the smart one, or the athletic one, or the creative and artistic one. Did you go to a school that had a particular reputation, for better or worse? And did that culture end up influencing the way that you saw yourself? If you went to the creative school, did creative skills become more important to you while you were there? Or did you choose that school because you valued creativity to begin with?

Understand that every group you belong to, every family member and friend you spend time with, and any news or media—all of this is influencing your truth. In all likelihood, the average direction that all of these are pointing you toward is the direction that your truth will lead you in. If your school or work, family, and friends all value creative expression, then you probably do too, and you may aspire to draw, write, or act to express this side of yourself.

However, what if there is a great divide? What if your family is organized, hardworking, and traditional, but your friends are wild, want to have fun, and not worry about anything. In this case, you have a choice to make. What is your truth, your path to live?

Living out our truth is not just an intellectual exercise. In some cases, we can decide to experiment with our lives, to try something new and see where it leads us. In other cases, we may not choose a particular route, instead deciding to live out different sides of ourselves.

When you value all of your groups—such as school, work, friends, family, clubs, etc., and you want to be liked by all of them, you may find yourself being different things to different people. To some extent, this is normal. We all have different roles. Someone may be a mother, daughter, spouse, and lawyer. These are all different roles that require different skills and approaches. And none of them necessarily conflict with the other. Someone who is motivated could meet all these obligations successfully.

However, there is a point where we may take things too far. You may find yourself behaving respectfully around your traditional parents. Yet with your wild friends, you may behave in a completely different way—blatantly disregarding the idea of respect altogether. Similarly, in front of teachers or your boss, you may behave and follow all the rules. Yet when they are not looking, you may look for opportunities to break all the rules that you can. When you are with your sporty friends, you talk and act like them, yet you morph into something else when you are with your creative and sensitive friends. You may change yourself to appease the crowds you happen to be with.

In such a case, who are you really? Are you different things to different people? Is it possible that some parts of yourself conflict? Perhaps your true nature is like the chameleon, and you feel like more of yourself when you can play different roles. However, if you feel torn apart and like you are just a phony actor, then it is time to rediscover a path toward your truth.

Some of these examples may apply to you, but perhaps not. Hopefully, you see that at some point, we can be stretched thin. We can try to be everything to everyone and lose who we are. When you lose yourself, this means you have not been walking the path of truth. You must seek it out once again and return to your true self.

What stops us from living our life is the fear that someone will not accept us for who we are, or that they will make fun of us, or fail to understand us, or simply criticize and judge us. We worry about these things, which can keep us stuck living someone else's truth rather than living our own.

The truth tends to be elusive because much of what we want conflicts with it. We may want to be liked, which can turn into wanting to be popular and then into wanting to be famous. Or we may want to buy something, which can turn into wanting to buy more expensive items, and then into wanting to be rich. Or we may want to feel better about our lives, which can turn into wanting to feel superior to others and then into wanting more and more power. Many of us have such wants, yet they tend to drive us away from truth.

To go a bit deeper into these examples, being popular or famous doesn't have any substance. Often, people who obsess over such things will be driven to live a lie because when we lie to people, we can get them to like us more quickly. We may lie and pretend to have the same motives, interests, and goals as other people, just to be accepted. Yet, the bonds and friendships we build are fake and brittle if we do that.

Similarly, when it comes to money, lying to people can provide a shortcut to get it faster.

With power, lying at strategic points or misrepresenting yourself in a more flattering way may help acquire more power.

Then we can see that popularity, money, and power are not necessarily false in themselves. But being attracted to them rather than to some greater good will tend to drive people away from truth.

Some of the most common things people have always wanted were just discussed: being popular or having money and power. In essence, much of society will be driven away from truth. They may even be taken so far away from it to the point where they will look in the mirror one day and no longer recognize the face they see.

Have you looked in the mirror lately? Do you know who is looking back at you?

Suppose many of the people we know are striving for popularity, money, and power. In that case, they may end up having little idea as to who they are. It's sad to say, but sometimes our pursuits can lead us directly toward falseness if we are not careful.

As a reminder, my goal here is to operate as a guide for you, to help you find the important truths for you. These are the truths that would help you live the life you were meant to live, which is the best life for you. Part of this role means warning you about the paths that may lead you away from your truth.

In my experience, popularity, money, and power are more meaningful and fulfilling when you acquire them due to living your truth, not by trying to get them directly.

Let's return to our core idea in this chapter. Why is the truth elusive? One key reason is that often, the people around you will be misguided. We tend to get fooled into thinking that they have it all figured out, but they rarely do. If you take advice from those who are lost themselves, then it is likely that you will find yourself lost as well, wandering away from the truth. Understand that just because most people in your life are following a path does not make that path correct. It doesn't make it the path that you were meant to go on.

Be careful before choosing to follow someone. You must first ask yourself: *Will this person lead me toward my truth or away from it? Do they even care about my truth?*

Something I learned long ago was that most people do *not* have it figured out. Most people have not found their truth. They may have seen bits and pieces of it, but not much more. They may have gotten a taste of their reality, but not much more. They may have seen the path they needed to take and started down it, but not much more.

Most of us live out the average truth of the closest people to us, such as friends, family, neighbors, and colleagues. Whatever they think, we think. Whatever they do, we do. We are like a mirror with the same thoughts, beliefs, desires, actions, and ultimately the same truths.

In some cases, this may be good and useful, but it could be holding us back in other cases.

Unfortunately, most of us are merely living out the most convenient truths that have been handed to us. Whether we discuss ethics, politics, or which values to live by, your truth may have just been what most people around you believed or whatever you were exposed to first.

We like to think that we are mapping out our own lives, figuring things out on our own. But are we really? Hasn't the path been conveniently laid out for us, and we just followed it? I make such comments here not to criticize but to urge us to think more deeply about our life's path. Is this convenient truth in front of us ours, or someone else's?

I want to be clear here that the path of convenience is not necessarily wrong. Most perspectives will have some truth in them. If your parents told you to work hard and stay out of trouble, how can anyone argue with this? Of course, it's good to work hard and stay out of trouble. But as easy as it is to agree with these ideas, it is also valuable to question them. You should always feel comfortable enough to question, to figure out the truth on your own and in your way.

If your parents advised you to work hard, consider what this truly means, "working hard." Some people work too hard and damage their body, or they fail to get enough rest and have an accident on the job. Some people work hard, but they make the same mistakes repeatedly, forcing them to work harder and longer to make up for it. They may work hard but accomplish very little.

Working hard can be a positive quality to have, but it depends on how we approach this.

And what does "stay out of trouble" mean? Sometimes you can't stay out of trouble. Sometimes trouble finds you—what do you do then? We are not told because trouble can come in quite a large variety of forms. It's difficult to be prepared for every kind of trouble that could arise. Our elders tell us to stay out of trouble with good reason. The best way to keep out of trouble is to avoid it altogether. Yet when trouble finds you, sometimes you have no choice but to become a part of it.

In alerting you that most of us accept the truths given to us, I do not want you to feel like you must rebel against all of the convenient ideas in your life. There likely is some ultimate truth in the perspectives you have been exposed to. You simply need to think it through on your own and perhaps test out what works for you. Stop assuming that a truth that was handed to you was indeed the ultimate truth.

Keep in mind that convenient truths are necessary for society to function. Imagine if a baby had never been exposed to any of the perspectives that we value in society. This would be like being lost in the woods. There would be no truth there. The baby's parents would not be there to protect, teach, or help. Without understanding what is true and without anyone to guide the baby along any truthful path, he would not survive. We need some convenient truths to serve as a starting point when we are young—but after this, we must pursue our own way.

For instance, some convenient truths could be to treat older people with respect, to share with friends, and that you should take responsibility for your actions. Suppose you were taught such things at school or by your parents. In that case, they are convenient because you simply followed them. Then you were rewarded for following them or punished for not doing so. I'm not implying that these are the wrong values to have. I'm just saying that they are convenient. They offer us an example of truths that the people around us hold and passed on to us.

Being exposed to different truths as you grow up is not so bad. It's a beautiful thing to be offered some direction in life.

But the absolute, universal truth remains elusive. Universal truths are principles or ideas that we believe always apply. These are ideas such as *I should always give people the benefit of the doubt*. Such a mindset works until that one time that you are taken advantage of. Another idea can be that *I should always do my best*. This mindset also works until you realize that always doing your best may cost you your health. Another idea is that *I am a highly talented artist, destined for fame and riches*. The theory makes sense until I meet an even more talented artist who decides that my work is not noteworthy at all.

When we think we have these universal truths, we are often wrong. It's better to understand that you only have a piece of the truth pie.

When you catch one part of the truth, the rest has escaped you. You have understood just one minor detail that applied in one case, at one point in time, but the rest has gone and slithered away like a snake.

You may think that you know the truth, but this is just because you can't know what you don't know.

You can't see what you haven't yet seen.

Understand that the path to truth is a journey. The truth tends to elude us, but it is still worth pursuing. The more truth you find, the more of You that you discover, and the more you become who you were truly meant to be.

Here is a warning about the truth that no one ever wants to admit.

Today, you will learn something that makes you think you have it all figured out. You will feel great, like you have finally uncovered the truth. Tomorrow, you will learn something that makes you question what you thought you knew. The next day you will realize that you were partly right to begin with, so not all is lost. Later on, you will question yourself once again, realizing that some things you thought made sense do not. Then, you will question your entire approach. Next, you will realize that you failed to consider something important, which forces you to start from the beginning again.

Then after years of hard work, something magical will happen.

The stars will align. You will have the grandest epiphany of all your life. You have no idea how you didn't see it before. Now, it is all clear. It was there all along, waiting for you to find it. The solution was so basic. You can't believe you had not thought of it before.

Everything you thought you knew before was ultimately wrong. Now, you hold the truth in your hands.

No, wait a second.

You made a mistake. You failed to consider something.

Okay, no problem, you take into account that part you had forgotten about, and now it all makes sense again.

You finally have it!

Until you don't—the truth slips from your fingers like grains of sand.

Then you have it again.

Then you don't.

In all your frustration, you decide to take a break.

Then, the break is over.

You work hard, get help, and make some progress.

After years of work, you feel like you are close to making a breakthrough.

The clouds are parting, and the sun is shining brighter than ever.

Maybe, just maybe, this time you have it? Who is to say?

This is the journey toward truth. When you think you have it, exercise caution.

The truth is elusive. Redirect yourself back toward it.

KEY QUESTIONS

The Truth is Elusive and We Must Redirect
Ourselves Back Toward It

1. What is it that you want if you quiet the voices of everyone else in your mind?
2. What is your natural feeling, emotion, belief, and action that you are inclined to perform before you consider what everyone else wants and expects from you?
3. Can you live as your true self right now, or is something steering you away from this?
4. Is there a truth about something you sincerely want to know, but it tends to escape you?
5. Right now, do you feel like you have your truth or that you are on the search for it?

TAKE ACTION TODAY

The Truth is Elusive and We Must Redirect
Ourselves Back Toward It

Action: **Today, go people-watching.** Look for someone who does not seem to be self-conscious at all. In other words, look for someone who is in their natural state. They may be going for a walk, reading, or browsing in a store. It doesn't matter what they are doing—just take notice.

Ask yourself: Is this a person who knows their personal truth, is this someone who is lost, or are they somewhere in between?

Attempt to look deeper into someone and see underneath the façade, titles, success, or failures of their lives.

Connect with someone, even if at a distance. What is their day like? What is their truth? How much can you learn about someone in a short period, just from observation? You may be surprised. By not knowing this person and not having a particular expectation, you may be in the position to observe his or her true self.

Reason: With this activity, hopefully, you will open your eyes and see that regardless of someone's appearance or status, often an individual will struggle to hold onto their truth. People who seem on top of the world in one setting can seem uncertain and lost in another—or vice versa. Every day, we only see the side of people that they choose to show us.

Tip: Observe at a distance in a way that does not interfere with what this person is doing. Do not follow someone to different locations—allow people to have their space. It helps to have something you appear to be doing, such as reading a book or having a snack. This way, you can appear as if you are not simply observing someone. And of course, if you make anyone uncomfortable, stop watching them.

We Must Know Ourselves Before We Can Know Anything Else

"A human being has so many skins inside, covering the depths of the heart. We know so many things, but we don't know ourselves! Why, thirty or forty skins or hides, as thick and hard as an ox's or bear's, cover the soul. Go into your own ground and learn to know yourself there."

— Meister Eckhart

In my search for truth, I came to this realization—*How could we know anything at all if we don't know ourselves?* Everything we are processing and understanding in this world happens through us. We tend to forget that the brain is part of the universe itself. And the brain is processing *everything*. We must attempt to understand the way our mind works so that we can understand ourselves and the universe.

The illusion we are presented with every day is one where we are learning objective information about the world around us. I see a baby, and I think that I am genuinely seeing that baby. I see a flower, and I believe that I actually see it—the same with the sun, with a bird, and with the floor beneath me.

No, I do not see these things for what they are. Everything that I see and perceive is coming through my senses and my perspective. Everything is filtered through me and how it impacts me. If I'm cold, the sun is great. If I'm hot, then I want to avoid the sun. The sun has not changed as much as my perspective has on a particular time of day.

When you learn your needs, wants, desires, thoughts, and habits and understand your perspective for what it is, you can begin to see the bigger truth out there. Learn the truth about yourself and who you are, and you will start to see the reality of the more expansive universe. Interestingly, the more you see that your ways are false and the limitations of your perspective, perhaps the closer to the truth you will get.

Understand that your mind is the key tool you use to perceive, and so you must learn at least some of the basics about how it works.

For example, an astronomer should be well educated on a telescope and how it works before using one. As powerful of a tool as it is, he will use it to see things that are incredibly far away, such as planets and asteroids. Trying to use one to see through objects or to see objects nearby would be ridiculous. This is not what it was designed to do.

Keep in mind that the brain is a tool from which we will attempt to make sense of everything else. You see something, and this is just a pattern of neurons firing in your brain. This pattern becomes your reality. You feel it in your brain and then your body as your reality. And maybe it is. Or perhaps it is just your unique perspective. You have to learn to see when there is a difference.

Up to here, I have mostly considered our conscious awareness, which is what the brain allows us to see. But there is plenty that is not available for us to see. There are parts of ourselves that we cannot access.

This is the subconscious. It is below our conscious awareness.

Since we have a subconscious that is largely ignored or unexplored, we must admit that we do not know ourselves very well.

How much of a person's experiences are in the subconscious? We cannot confirm it, for these parts are not accessible to us. It may be 10%, or 50%, or 90%. Perhaps some people who have suffered trauma hide some of these experiences or related thoughts and feelings in their subconscious. Ultimately, the subconscious is there to protect us from hurtful truths.

Now, let us consider this: How well do you know yourself? It is a fundamental question, but not so easy to answer. I have just told you that an unknown part of ourselves is in the subconscious. If that is the case, it's difficult to be sure how well we even know ourselves.

Then let's simplify the question. How well do you know your conscious self? Even here, we may find that we do not know as much as we think we do.

We like to think that we know and understand ourselves, but have you ever been placed in an unexpected or novel situation? Did you react differently than you would have expected? This probably happened because you had no prior experiences from which to judge what to do. You may have ended up reacting based on emotion, intuition, or instinct. In the end, perhaps you overreacted, or you may have even felt overwhelmed and frozen in place instead of taking action.

Most of us live in ordinary or expected circumstances, day by day. We generally know what we will face, and we know how we tend to respond to these events. We know ourselves as long as we are dealing with ordinary and everyday circumstances. But we rarely know ourselves in situations that push us to our limits.

When you are put in a situation outside of what you would normally expect, you can meet a new you. This can be good or bad, of course. I think it's good to push ourselves beyond our comfort zone. Still, everyone has limits, and pushing too far can be traumatizing, so that is to be avoided.

Consider some of these boundary-pushing circumstances. Imagine if this happened to you:

- You inherit 10 million dollars unexpectedly.
- You are at an ATM, and someone pulls a knife on you and tells you to give them the money.
- You find yourself lost in the middle of the wilderness. You have no food, water, or shelter.
- A stranger on the streets belittles and harasses you and won't stop following you—you have done nothing to provoke this.
- You win a Nobel prize, a MacArthur "genius" grant, or the highest award anyone could attain in your field.
- You are having dinner at a fancy restaurant, and a stranger starts spitting on the food of people at your table.
- You are in intense competition, and you are about to win when you fail horribly at the last moment (e.g., you are running a marathon and you trip and fall, and someone else wins.)
- You are walking to work when you see that a school is on fire. There are hundreds of children inside, oblivious that the building is burning. The fire is blazing, and no one is doing anything about it.
- Your bank account is depleted with no explanation, and no one at your bank can figure out what the problem is.

Do you know what you would do in these cases? Sometimes we think we know, but we don't until we are faced with different situations that push us to our limits.

And we arrive at a critical point here. You may be able to figure out your truth more quickly when you push yourself to the limits. It is not essential to do this in *all* areas of your life. But it may make sense to challenge yourself more in *some* of the most important areas to you. Of course, sometimes life can push you to the limits whether you ask for it or not.

For example, perhaps you just received a great job opportunity out of the blue, but it is in another state. You are excited and decide you will go ahead and move. When your best friend finds out about this, she is unhappy and mad at you. She feels like you are betraying her by moving. However, your truth is telling you that you need to explore a new place and a new job to live up to your life's potential. This friendship may be one of the most critical relationships in your life, yet you may decide to allow it to be tested. As close as this friend is, you need to go on this journey for yourself.

Perhaps your friend becomes quite upset and has a hard time accepting that you have chosen to abandon her, at least from her perspective. Of course, if this friend is worth keeping, you should find a way to make amends and stay in contact. In the end, if the friendship could not survive you moving away, then perhaps it was time to make new friends. You may want to avoid having friends who will only hold you back, preventing you from living your truth.

Understand that everything you learn and everything you experience is processed through your self. This is obvious, isn't it? But consider this more deeply. Everything is processed and filtered through your mind, emotions, feelings, beliefs, thoughts, prior experiences, desires, and goals. Anything that you read, see, or experience is filtered through your self. For that reason, you must get to know yourself.

Learn to be aware of your own biases, as these will guide you away from truth. For example, if you admire and look up to someone, you may fail to see anything wrong that they do. You may assume that they are right about everything and blindly follow their truth rather than pursuing your own. Instead, it is better to explore yourself to understand your viewpoints and limitations. This way, you will be able to see the bigger truth.

While exploring and figuring out your truth, be cautious if there are people around you who are very adamant about pursuing their truth. We all have the right to pursue our truth, but sometimes people are too forceful, and they forget to consider your truth as well. Listen to their truth and keep it in mind but do not allow it to drown out your will and spirit.

As a note of caution, pay attention if there are people in your life who insist that you live by their truth. Be aware if there are groups you belong to that do not care about your truth, and they only care about how much you believe in theirs. If that happens, you may be guided away from your personal truth, as you become limited by their ways of perceiving. Instead, it will be more fruitful to pursue your own way.

In seeking your truth, realize that you do not have the whole picture. The complete picture is forever unfolding in front of us, in this reality, in this universe. And when we think we have captured it, it changes on us. The universe is not static—it is evolving, changing, and adapting.

You should be careful if you feel too strongly that you already have the truth. Feeling this way will present obstacles toward finding more of your reality. It's healthy to have some doubt, for this way, you can be open to explore, learn, and discover more of the truth that is still waiting for you.

Understand this: in getting to know yourself more deeply, you will be in a better position to identify the actual truth. However, the biggest mistake you can make is to assume that your single perspective is the one and entire truth. Instead, it is just one part of the truth pie. That is all.

Remember to be wary of truths that feel too easy—the ones that everyone around you believe, the ones your parents insist on, or your manager, or your peers. Their perspectives are not necessarily false—but question whether their views deserve to be a part of your truth. If you find yourself believing in all the convenient facts—for example, if they make you feel good about yourself, or it is simply easier to agree with the people around you, then you must take a step back and question these.

If you do not question them publicly, at least do this for yourself.

Often, we are surrounded by stories in our day-to-day lives. We just don't realize that this is what they are. We confuse these convenient stories as being the truth. Instead of being the truth, they tend to have *some* truth in them. Stories may convince people to take action, make people feel like they are part of a group, or believe in something. However, they rarely provide you with the whole truth.

Consider the stories in your life and the truths or falseness in them. Are there stories you tell yourself about yourself? About others? How accurate are those stories?

For most of the stories people tell, they present themselves as heroes. Whoever writes history is often the one who comes out as the hero. Is this truth, or just a matter of perspective? Of course, when you find one group that believes one thing and another group that thinks the opposite, this is usually a matter of perspective. In the end, both groups may hold part of the truth.

Do you know what you want to get out of life? Do you know your most deeply held truths? If you do, is this something that you gleefully tell the world? Sometimes, it's best to keep this knowledge to yourself.

It's important to know what you want. But consider that often these wants present a vulnerability, a weak spot for someone to jump in and tell you what you want to hear. When they tell you what you want to hear, they can manipulate you to get what they want.

If you want a long-term relationship, for example, someone may learn this and then pretend to be whatever it is that they think you want. They may do this even if they prefer a short-term relationship, simply because they believe it is best to be liked. In your pursuit of the truth, you should understand that some people have no problem lying to get what they want.

When we know what we want, we have to be honest with ourselves. But we should also consider *not* laying this out for the world to see. If you trust someone or love someone, then, of course, you can share your heart with them.

Otherwise, it can be worthwhile to develop a poker face and *not* broadcast to the world what you think is the truth or what you want. When people conveniently offer the road to what you want, it may be so that they can take advantage of you, to get what they want from you. When you have a poker face, they will not know precisely what you want, and so they may reveal more of their true selves to you.

In this life, others will try to offer a road map to whatever it is you want. But what if we don't even know what we want?

Remember the main idea of this section: **We must know ourselves before we can know anything else.**

This may be a challenging idea to comprehend fully, but let's consider some examples of how this can play out.

Suppose you have never been loved, or you have never loved someone. How can you read Shakespeare or literature that centers around this topic and truly understand it? How can you see people in love in the streets and know what they are feeling? Of course, to know love, you should give it, accept it, and explore what this means in your own life. You must experience what love is if you can ever hope to comprehend it in the world around you.

This is how it works for so many parts of life. It isn't just with love. For instance, let's consider violence. At some point, even if it is when you were a child, you may have acted out in violence. You may have become frustrated that you did not get what you wanted, and you decided to hit or push someone. By enacting this behavior, you learned that you had a part of yourself that could become violent. You realized that you could become angry or impulsive.

And in exploring some of these parts of yourself, perhaps you were able to understand better how violence can happen in the world. It may be because someone wanted something badly, and they did not get it. It may be because someone didn't have adults in their lives to monitor them and teach them that this behavior was wrong (outside of self-defense, at least). You may have felt when a great injustice happened around you that possibly you could resort to violence.

Regardless of whether you view violence as acceptable in some cases or not, you likely can understand how some people would resort to this. Even if you prefer not to act on such feelings, you have probably experienced some emotions that can lead to violence—envy, anger, selfishness, impulsiveness, and so on.

With having seen violence, having felt the urge to hit or push, perhaps even having been hit or shoved yourself at some point, you understand what it is. Now you can read about wars or vengeful attacks, and you can comprehend on some level why it is happening, even if you disagree with it. But if you didn't know this in yourself, how would you understand it in the world around you?

We all know that violence is not acceptable, morally. We learn this as children in school. But it is still a reality of life. If we can begin to understand our violent nature (even if we do not act on it), then we may come to know why or how violence exists in the world.

Ultimately, I believe that we know things about the world because we know them about ourselves. For the weather, trees, birds, or the sun, these are all things that are processed and filtered through our mind, thoughts, beliefs, desires, prior experiences, and actions.

When you see a tree, it is processed through your eyes, brain, knowledge, and understanding of them, your feelings about trees, your beliefs about them, and your prior experiences. We tend to forget if you touch a tree, all of your experiences with it happen in your mind. Sure, the tree exists out there in the real world—it is not just in your imagination, but how you experience that tree is unique to you. You can only know that tree as well as you know yourself in the end.

Perhaps the tree has its soul and will, but if you do not know your own soul and will, how can you discover it in the tree or other life around you? Suppose you do not allow yourself to feel emotional about anything. Then how can you empathize with someone else's feelings or a tree's dilemmas?

We share many experiences with a tree—we grow, can live to old age, nourish ourselves with water, and can benefit from sunlight.

Here is an insightful passage that may help you to see trees differently, and in turn, could help you to see yourself more deeply:

> "For me, trees have always been the most penetrating preachers. I revere them when they live in tribes and families, in forests and groves. And even more I revere them when they stand alone. They are like lonely persons. Not like hermits who have stolen away out of some weakness, but like great, solitary men, like Beethoven and Nietzsche. In their highest boughs the world rustles, their roots rest in infinity; but they do not lose themselves there, they struggle with all the force of their lives for one thing only: to fulfill themselves according to their own laws, to build up their own form, to represent themselves. Nothing is holier, nothing is more exemplary than a beautiful, strong tree." — Herman Hesse, *Bäume. Betrachtungen und Gedichte* (Trees. Reflections and Poems)

The more you know yourself, the better you will understand the tree. And by taking the time to get to know a tree, you will come to know yourself more deeply.

Now, let's consider some other thoughts and questions that can help us understand ourselves even further.

How much do you know about the human eye? About the brain? Your soul? Or about your desires? How much do you know about your motivations? How do you feel about your life?

What do you believe and think about the world and its state—where did you get this information? Was it given to you, or did you process this on your own? Did you focus on facts, or did you focus on conclusions other people had come to? Were the "facts" conveniently given to you, or did you work to process them and analyze them on your own?

How much do you know about why you desire what you desire? What do you know about your conscious and subconscious? What about dreams— why do you dream what you dream? What do you know about DNA— your genetic programming?

What about your personality? Where did this come from? Are there things that happened to you before you can even remember that affected who you ultimately became?

Do you ever think about who you are, or do you just accept it? Do you allow yourself to be as you are, or are you trying to make yourself into who you want to be? Do you view yourself as something static or as an organic, growing being that is becoming something? And what are you becoming?

How deep is your human experience? Is there great depth in your life, or is it just superficial in the end? How deeply have you experienced different emotions and feelings such as love, hate, generosity, greed, happiness, sadness, pride, shame, excitement, and anger?

Where do your thoughts come from? Are these just automated processes that you cannot truly control? Are you in control of your thoughts, or are they coming from beyond you, and you just receive them, or feel them as your own?

Then, what is good thinking? How can you know if your thought processes are sound and worthwhile? Perhaps most of your thinking is not so sharp, leading you to make terrible decisions in your life. How would you know? If your critical thinking skills are weak, you probably would not realize that this is the case, right?

Consider emotions. Which ones do you tend to experience the most? Are you often sad, angry, hopeful, happy, or anxious? Are you unemotional? Are your emotions easily accessible to yourself, or are they hidden away? Do you confront, deny, or ignore them? Do you feel them deeply and allow them to pass, or hold onto them until it agonizes you? Where are these emotions coming from?

Are you rational, intuitive, creative, questioning, demanding, persistent, or apathetic? What describes you? Is there a single word that can represent you? A phrase?

What is understanding? Is this something that you know when you have it? Or is this fleeting? Can you know something through just emotion, intuition, or reason, or do you need more? Is your mind just identifying patterns and associations, or does it understand something? Does it just think it is making sense of life, or is it actually making sense of it? How would you know the difference?

Are your thoughts, beliefs, feelings, desires, and behaviors truly your own, or are they just the average of the five closest people in your life?

Are you your own separate being, or are you part of a continuum or chain of being? For example, are you an extension of your parents? Are you reincarnated, having always been here? Or are you a unique individual?

How much can you know? How much is worth knowing?

How deeply have you contemplated who you are?

Are you a stranger to yourself, or do you know who you are?

Are you conscious or just going through processes that give you the illusion of thinking, feeling, and knowing?

Is this all just a grand illusion?

Who are you?

Do you know?

And if you do not know, who could possibly know?

When faced with a new situation, do you know what you are going to do about it? How do you decide what to do? Who taught you this?

Who taught you to be yourself and to be human?

Are you being You, or just the human that you were taught to be? Is being a human being something that we do on our own, or do we need to be taught to be one?

If we need to be taught this, then why is that the case? Do all animals need to be taught to be themselves?

Can a lion raised by a goat grow up thinking it is a goat? Or will its lion nature come out in the end?

What is the inner essence and nature of who you are that no one else can live out? Only you can do it.

No matter what you learn about psychology, biology, history, anthropology, philosophy, self-development, or religion, how much will this tell you about yourself in the end?

Your self can reasonably only be explored through yourself. You may study psychology and learn about yourself and some terminology that can help you process what your inner experience is all about. Still, ultimately, the only way to explore your self is through yourself. Even if you get the aid of a coach or therapist, they will help you to learn about yourself through your own words, feelings, and actions. They will help you to identify patterns that perhaps you had missed.

Consider that as human societies, we put tremendous effort into mapping out different fields. Cartographers have mapped out the planet that we live on. Anatomists have mapped out every human organ and its function. Physicists have worked on mapping out the rules and nature of the universe we live in. Ornithologists have worked on mapping out every kind of bird in existence. In many fields, it seems that we focus on mapping out all the knowledge that we can.

Yet, how do we map out the self? Psychology can map out many different aspects of the mind, consciousness, and behavior. Still, some concepts may pertain more to some people than others. For example, much of psychology has historically focused on problems of the psyche and behavior, such as identifying disorders and symptoms. One psychologist may focus on sex (e.g., Sigmund Freud), another may focus on spirituality (e.g., Carl Jung), self-actualization (Abraham Maslow), or childhood (Jean Piaget).

Some of these psychologists may have simply been exploring their inner nature and then come up with theories that reflected this. If this is true, they may have missed out on essential features of what it means to be you. Perhaps they captured some critical parts of what it means to be human but still missed something that makes you who you are.

The topics that psychology has followed may or may not be the ones that pertain to you and your truth. Even if psychologists have explored some important topics, you must ask how much they apply to your unique circumstance.

Being human is fascinating because, on some level, we are all just the same. Still, on another level, our individuality makes us distinct from every other person who ever lived.

Take the time to discover what it is that makes you, you.

KEY QUESTIONS

We Must Know Ourselves Before We
Can Know Anything Else

1. How well do you know different parts of yourself: emotional, intellectual, spiritual, physical, creative, etc.? Are there certain weak spots that you should focus on understanding more deeply?
2. Who is your best friend? Could you learn something about yourself from speaking to him or her?
3. Think of some of the most significant decisions you made in your life. Knowing what you know now, would you have done something differently? How have you changed?
4. What is something you learned early in life that is *not* a part of your truth? How did you unlearn this, or how could you?
5. What is a personal truth that you could admit is just your unique perspective—it is not necessarily the truth for everyone else.

TAKE ACTION TODAY

We Must Know Ourselves Before We
Can Know Anything Else

I had a friend who told me that when he was nine years old, his teacher got concerned when she realized that he was missing from class, so she looked for him. After some time, she finally found him in the bathroom. He had been staring at himself in the mirror. The strange part was that he was there for an hour, trying to connect with his soul by gazing at his reflection. It was the first time in his life that he realized he did not know himself.

Action: **Today, I want you to look at yourself in the mirror. Gaze into your reflection and ask yourself some questions.**

As a reminder, here are a few questions I asked earlier in this chapter for you to reflect on (or you may choose to reflect on your own life's questions):

- How much do you know about *why* you desire what you desire?
- How deep is your human experience?
- Are you a good thinker?
- What emotions do you tend to have?
- Are you rational, intuitive, creative, questioning, demanding, persistent, or apathetic?
- Is there a single word that can describe you? A phrase?
- Are your thoughts, beliefs, feelings, desires, and behaviors truly your own, or are they just the average of the five closest people in your life?

This task can be uncomfortable, but that is okay. When you look in the mirror, are you hung up on superficial concerns, such as how you look? Or can you look further into a deeper part of your true self? Even though this is a visual task, do not get stuck on appearances. I would encourage you to explore your feelings. When you look at your facial expressions, what is the feeling, emotion, or concern that underlies them? Whether your face is relaxed or rigid, what is the reason?

Reason: We spend most of our lives looking outward, not inward. Looking into the mirror and asking questions can help you reflect on who you are, what you want out of life, and also to connect with yourself. There may be parts of ourselves that are hidden or neglected, and we should strive to acknowledge and understand our authentic selves.

Tip: Try to imagine that you are looking at someone else, not yourself. What do you think of this person that you are looking at in the mirror? What do you think that they feel about you? While I encourage you to get in touch with your emotions and feelings, you can also consider your thoughts, memories, beliefs, desires, and plans.

Identify Your Values to Use as an Inner Compass That Illuminates Your True Path

"The major value in life is not what you get. The major value in life is what you become. That is why I wish to pay fair price for every value. If I have to pay for it or earn it, that makes something of me. If I get it for free, that makes nothing of me."

— Jim Rohn

A way to know yourself and stop having your truth escape from you is to identify your values. Have you ever taken some time to explore what your most deeply held values are?

Think about it: What is the most important thing of all in your life?

Does the question produce no immediate answer? Perhaps you can think of many values, but you are not sure how you would order them. Maybe they all seem important.

I have found that it is paramount to know your top five values or so. These values will form your inner compass, from which you will be able to navigate your life toward your truth. (For a list of 100 values, see the end of this chapter.)

Imagine this: You are a ship's captain, navigating the unknown waters of your life. Without a compass, you will remain lost. Here, your compass will not be in cardinal directions. North, South, East, and West do not matter. Instead, to steer this ship, you will need your four or five cardinal values to lead the way.

I urge you—get a hold of your values. Know what they are. Do this now, or after reading this chapter, or after reading *Your Personal Truth.* But either way, do it.

Soon, you may come across new, uncharted territory, and you may not know what to do. Perhaps you will find that when a situation is uncertain, you just freeze. When this happens, you can pause and regain your senses and pull out your inner compass of values.

For tricky life situations, it can help to rank order your top values. This may be difficult, but try. To do this, imagine scenarios, or think back to life experiences you have had, where one value competed with another. Which value was more important to you in the end. And which one could you afford to sacrifice, if needed?

Ranking your values may seem like just busy work, but it is not. When you know your values, you will be much closer to figuring out your truth. Take a minute to identify some values you hold, and then you can examine them more closely. Is the value that you think is most important indeed the most important one? Have you lost your way and been giving too much time, attention, and energy to something that is not very important to you?

Notice any mismatch between what you think you value and how you live your life. Where are the contradictions? Some may say they value honesty, yet they will lie often and tell the truth rarely in an ordinary day. Some may say they desire peace yet slam doors and raise their voice at the slightest provocation. Others claim to value intelligence but leap into making major life choices without considering their options and their likely consequences.

In your life, ask yourself where the mismatch is.

A good question to ask yourself is where most of your time is spent. Do you value family time yet hardly ever see them because you are working too much? Or do you value work but find yourself distracted by social media for extended periods?

When I find that I have strayed from my primary values and priorities in life, I force myself to log where my time is going. I will write down what I was doing every minute of the day. Try that, and then ask if too much time went wasted on activities of little value. Or was some time spent in a counterproductive way, working against your goals and values? You may be surprised to find that what you think matters and what you spend your time on is entirely different.

As humans, we are complex, so I urge you to explore your values logically. Perhaps you think that you value health, but you smoke, or you never exercise, or you often speed when you drive and do not wear a seatbelt.

It is a challenge to live consciously and to perceive our own lives objectively. We have all kinds of psychological devices to make ourselves feel safe and comfortable. But as I value truth, I prefer to avoid being blissfully ignorant. Suppose I am living in contradiction to my values or opposing them some-how. In that case, I need to ask myself if I can change something to live by my values more fully. As an alternative, I can ask if perhaps something that I thought I valued was not so important to me after all.

I would like to provide you with an example of finding a contradiction in my values. Many, many years ago, I was extremely impatient with my mother. I knew consciously that this was unfair and that she did not de-serve this. I felt horrible about my behavior and was not happy with myself. But sometimes, I felt like I could not control myself. I would suddenly get angry and impatient, and I would yell at her. Most of the time, I was perfectly calm and composed, but that was not good enough. I would have these outbursts and later realize that it had been for something trivial. There was no reason for it.

This had become a regular occurrence, unfortunately.

The way I was able to change this negative pattern was to realize that there were so many other values that outshined my need to be right or my need to have things now. Being right or having things now meant nothing if I would strain a relationship or cause my mother to be stressed or unhappy. She has always been a wonderful mother and did her best to raise me, supporting and encouraging me up to the present day.

I eventually asked myself, why would I be so nasty to a person who I love and who loves me? Why would I even consider behaving this way?

That was the issue—I wasn't considering it. Instead, I was acting impulsively, not having evaluated what I was doing. I had behaved this way because I was valuing needing to be correct and needing things now. If someone contradicted me or did not give me something I wanted right away, then I could lose all my patience, get angry, and yell.

Then, when I met my wife (back when we were starting to date), I realized that I was perpetuating this pattern. I was treating her poorly too. I was yelling without any good reason, and our relationship was beginning to suffer before it had truly begun. She told me: "This needs to change, or I won't be here long."

Of course, this was a motivating force. But interestingly, I found that it was not so difficult to grow and undo this horrible pattern of mine. All I needed to do was realize that the value I had for my relationship was magnitudes higher than the value I had for my need to be right or to have things now. I was able to retrain myself and see that I valued my family, relationship, peace, and integrity. I never *really* cared about being right and have things now when I thought of it. Instead, I valued intelligence, empathy, patience, and fairness—when I realized this, I made changes in my life.

But again, it's not that difficult to change when you know your values. Think of it. If you truly value something, why would it be so hard to live by it? Our values just tend to get mixed up, or we forget which ones are important. But if we consider them deeply, and remember what we truly value, then we should be able to live by them.

To put this as simply as possible. When you say you value something but do not follow through on this with your actions, you are essentially lying. All we have to do is stop lying.

Values aren't just something that you write on a piece of paper and then forget about them. I needed to learn to live by my values. I needed to embody my values in my thoughts and actions every day. I needed to stop lying.

I hope you think through any contradictions in your life and start to question what your values are. Perhaps you have also been living by values that did not represent your true self. Only you can see this and overcome your bad habits to find your direction once again.

As a final tip to help you identify your most authentic values, consider how much you may value something once it is gone. In life, we often forget to consider that the people, abilities, opportunities, or things that are here today may be gone tomorrow. How much will you value something once it is gone, damaged, or no longer within your grasp?

As an example, if your sense of hearing suddenly stopped working correctly, how much would you value it then? Months ago, I was exposed to excessive construction noise outside of my apartment, day after day, for weeks. I realized too late that I should have been wearing earplugs, and I was left with some ringing in one ear. Fortunately, through time, my ear has improved gradually.

Nonetheless, this experience made me realize that I needed to be more careful and value the senses and abilities that I had. I now avoid exposure to loud noises to make sure to protect my ears. I even carry earplugs in case I find myself in a setting with excessive noise.

Again—it is when we are threatened with losing something that we come to comprehend its value.

Alternatively, you may think that you value something very highly. But if it disappeared from your life, would it truly affect you? If not, then maybe it wasn't as valuable as you thought it was. For example, perhaps you value your job tremendously. But if you were fired suddenly, it could be that your skills are in high enough demand that you would quickly find a new one if necessary. Within months, you may even forget about your old position. You may then find that the actual value was not in any single job but in the high qualifications you possessed.

What do you value?

Below is a list of 100 values I would like you to explore and consider. Take a minute to read through the list and think about which ones you value the most.

1.	Acceptance	19.	Decisiveness
2.	Achievement	20.	Dignity
3.	Adaptability	21.	Diligence
4.	Adventure	22.	Dreaming
5.	Authenticity	23.	Efficiency
6.	Authority	24.	Elegance
7.	Balance	25.	Empathy
8.	Beauty	26.	Environmentalism
9.	Boldness	27.	Ethics
10.	Compassion	28.	Exploration
11.	Challenge	29.	Fairness
12.	Charm	30.	Faith
13.	Community	31.	Family
14.	Composure	32.	Forgiveness
15.	Confidence	33.	Freedom
16.	Courage	34.	Friendship
17.	Creativity	35.	Fun
18.	Curiosity	36.	Generosity

37. Gratitude
38. Growth
39. Guidance
40. Happiness
41. Harmony
42. Health
43. Heroism
44. Honesty
45. Honor
46. Humor
47. Impact
48. Imagination
49. Independence
50. Inspiration
51. Intelligence
52. Intuition
53. Justice
54. Kindness
55. Knowledge
56. Leadership
57. Learning
58. Love
59. Loyalty
60. Mastery
61. Maturity
62. Mindfulness
63. Nature
64. Openness
65. Optimism
66. Order
67. Passion
68. Patience
69. Peace
70. Popularity
71. Power
72. Practicality

73. Relaxation
74. Religion
75. Resilience
76. Resourcefulness
77. Respect
78. Responsibility
79. Science
80. Security
81. Self-control
82. Selflessness
83. Self-reliance
84. Self-respect
85. Sensitivity
86. Service
87. Simplicity
88. Speed
89. Spirituality
90. Strength
91. Success
92. Thoughtfulness
93. Timeliness
94. Traditionalism
95. Truth
96. Uniqueness
97. Wealth
98. Wisdom
99. Wonder
100. Work

A key topic we have discussed is that we must know ourselves before we can find our truth. Well, beyond knowing our values, how can we get to know ourselves more deeply? This is an important question that we will now consider.

In the following chapters, we will discuss the path to knowing your true self. This involves five key elements: 1) remembering yourself, 2) uncovering yourself, 3) recovering yourself, 4) discovering yourself, and 5) creating yourself.

KEY QUESTIONS

Identify Your Values to Use as an Inner
Compass That Illuminates Your True Path

1. What are your most deeply held values (use the list above for inspiration)?
2. What is something you have been valuing, spending too much time and energy on, that you would like to reduce or remove from your life?
3. Are there other values you find important, which were not in the list above? Which ones are they?
4. When you think of your top few values, consider if you are contradicting any of these in your life. How can you become more congruent with yourself?
5. What is something many people around you tend to value but you don't think is quite so important?

┤ TAKE ACTION TODAY ├

Identify Your Values to Use as an Inner
Compass That Illuminates Your True Path

Action: **Using the list of values provided above, come up with your list of 3-7 critical values in your life.** When you have them, attempt to rank them. It's okay if you are not entirely sure but do your best. You can always think about your list of values and reorganize it later on.

When you have your list in rank order, **ask yourself if this represents how you are living your life.** Are you putting your #1 value first in your life, above everything else? Are you putting time and energy into these values every day? Are there unimportant or trivial things that you are making time for every day while neglecting some of your highest values?

If you are living by your values, then this is wonderful. But for many people, it is a struggle to live by them every day. Which values are you struggling to live by? What can you change?

It will also help to consider why your chosen values are so important to you. Why these values and not others?

Reason: The better you know your values, the better you will know yourself. In knowing your values, you will make better life decisions and make them more efficiently, as they will be more likely to stay true to yourself.

Tip: Reflect on some activities you enjoy or what you tend to spend most of your time on. You can also consider what you wish you had more time to do. Otherwise, think about what you would like to produce or attract more of in your life. When you have these in mind, consider which values they may represent. For example, if you make it a point to stay in touch with old friends, then this means you put a high value on Relationships or Communication.

Also, don't worry if your values are not listed above. You can choose your own or rephrase them in your own words if you wish.

Remember Yourself

"Remember who you are and where
you come from; otherwise, you don't
know where you are going."

— Karolína Kurková

How can we remember who we are? The best way to do this is to listen to your heart. Now the key is to consider what that means. Essentially, the real you is not what we see, nor all that you have been taught to think and do. There is a deeper part of yourself.

I believe many of us get used to going against our spirit, and we have to *remember* who we are. This is easier said than done.

I have come to think that part of our human journey is that we lose ourselves along the way. Many well-meaning people in our lives teach us so much that we may lose our core, authentic self in time. We develop obsessions—whether making money, seeking fame, having a perfect figure, or an addiction to buying stuff or playing games. This is where the world is steering us, away from ourselves.

The modern world is excellent at filling our lives with distractions that do not necessarily lead to a truthful, meaningful place.

Notice that animals have powerful drives, which we call instincts. To me, instinct is just knowing who you are. You know that when something happens, you react in a certain way, and you don't need to question it because it is a deep drive inside yourself—it is you. Yet, when placed in zoos, animals start to lose their instincts. Animals that may have had a killer instinct can lose it. They can lose who they are, trapped behind bars. This is because the zoo is an artificial environment, holding back their true, wild selves.

Interestingly, I have come to think that humans also have a wild side that has been lost. It makes sense, of course, for society to avoid any part of ourselves that may cause havoc or violence, especially without any good reason. But as all animals have a wild side, and we are animals, perhaps we have this side to ourselves too, and it is neglected.

As part of our *domestication* on becoming human, we go to school and obey a teacher's instructions. Then, later on, most of us go to work and obey our boss's instructions. If we are promoted to management, we continue to follow the lead manager's instructions. We are taught from the earliest phases in our lives that we must respect order. We are just a tiny puzzle piece in a much bigger puzzle.

If we had a wild side, we tended to lose it. But it's not a matter of "if." Just look at young children and how wild and carefree they can be. Perhaps without society to teach them to be civilized humans, they would have grown into wild adults.

Think back: If you stepped out of line in your youth at any time, someone was there to correct you and show you the error of your ways. I can still recall being a child and constantly hearing the words "single-file line." Of course, in elementary school, teachers said this to remind us to walk in a precise, straight line on the way to the bathroom. They did not want to see disorder.

And so we learned to stay in line, to be orderly, follow instructions, and the wild parts of us were stamped out. Maybe some of this is good, but perhaps not all of it.

If we can learn to appreciate the wild nature in the world, why shouldn't we enjoy it in ourselves? Why shouldn't we appreciate the wild side of humanity? Must we follow the rules and instructions perfectly all of the time? You may explore such ideas as you figure out your truth.

Every day we are led along certain paths. Our teachers showed us that we had to follow their instructions as they reminded us to "stay in line." We are adults now, but perhaps not much has changed. We don't talk back to superiors, say something that could make someone feel uncomfortable, or laugh at inappropriate times. This is just what adults do (or don't do).

Consider this: Do you deny parts of who you are just to follow the expected order? Is that order worth it? Or are you making a personal sacrifice?

If you choose to deny your true nature every day, you may eventually find that you do not know who you are anymore. You may have been following the paths others laid out for you for so long. For example, those paths the people around you believed to be good and encouraged you to go on. Perhaps all that this will accomplish is introduce falseness in your life and lead you away from your truth.

Ask yourself: Have I forgotten who I truly am? Have I been masquerading as someone that I am not? Am I an imposter in my own life?

No one can answer such questions except for you. Only you know if you are where you were meant to be. Even if you are not where you wanted to be, then the key question is whether you are doing everything you can to find that path that you were meant to be on.

Are you committed to being your true self? Is this something you are willing to struggle for? To take seriously? Or will you calmly lose the battle for yourself and allow your mind and body to be guided wherever the forces of the world happen to take you?

If you have forgotten who you were, how can you recapture yourself and remember? You may contact childhood friends or family members that you have not seen in a long time. Or you could get in touch with some lost beliefs, values, or desires that you had long ago and had set aside.

When was the last time that you felt completely free to be your true self? Were you a child? A teenager? A young adult? Was it decades ago, a few years ago, or months ago? Is it just on the weekends when you're alone? Or does it only happen when you are around close friends and family?

Sometimes remembering isn't enough, and you must get in touch with who you were, at that last point where you can recall having been your true self. Maybe you have lost touch with family—and you must visit them. Perhaps you have lost touch with a topic or activity you loved, and you must do this again. Or maybe you have denied a part of your personality to please someone, and it is time that you go back to being your true self.

Remembering who you are doesn't just mean revisiting memories. It involves recapturing who you are for yourself. When you remember, you can find your true self inside yourself, in your mind, and then you will know the right path for you.

KEY QUESTIONS

Remember Yourself

1. Did you used to be a different person? If so, did you change for better or worse?
2. Do you find that pretending, lying, or exaggerating is a regular part of your life? If so, why are you covering up who you are?
3. When you were a child, what excited you the most? Do you still gain some pleasure in this?
4. Have you stifled a part of yourself that is wild, rebellious, or spontaneous to keep the peace?
5. Do you feel like the true you is different from what you have chosen to show the world?

TAKE ACTION TODAY

Remember Yourself

Action: **Consider the last time that you felt like things were going your way.** You were happy, you were loved, or you felt generally fulfilled in life. Embrace this positive feeling that you had at that time in your life. **Then, ask why you felt that way.** Was it because of the people you had in your life? Was it because of a particular event that happened? Had you just achieved a life goal?

If you struggle to think of such a time, it could help to talk to an old friend to discuss some memories or to look through some old photos.

When you have your memory, relive the experience in your mind. Consider: did you have a positive feeling because you had so much potential then? Was it a simpler time? Were you more sure of what you wanted?

Is there a way to recapture that feeling? Instead of just recalling a memory, can you revisit a location that connects to your heart? Or can you contact people who inspired you or perform an activity you used to love but had given up on?

Reason: The goal here is simply to remember yourself. It's easy to forget who we are and how we got to the point we are at now. Sometimes, we need to step back and remember when things were going our way and we felt like our true selves.

Tip: Instead of just reconnecting with an experience in your mind, can you recreate it? Can you play the music that reminds you of a time and place? If something inspired you in the past, can you draw from that same source once again?

Uncover Yourself

"What I've found—and the older I get, the
more I understand this and stand behind
it—is, my whole life has been an exploration
of telling the truth. It's scary to be truthful,
and it's scary to reveal yourself, and I'm very
attracted to doing things that scare me."

— Jane Wiedlin

Now that you have remembered yourself, I need you to be brave, and you must uncover yourself.

Imagine being in a building and an earthquake happens, and all of this concrete mess falls on you. You are weak but still conscious. You must work hard to get all of this heaviness, rubble, and debris off of you.

This scenario is just a metaphor, where the true meaning is that you must uncover all of this baggage that has held you back to get to your true self.

Consider: Have certain ideas led you along the wrong path? Perhaps certain beliefs, people, thoughts, desires, or feelings have led you astray? What has been covering you up, blocking yourself from yourself? Are you worried or scared that people will realize something about you? Are you too concerned with what other people will think?

Have you been living a lie because it will help to make other people happy? Perhaps this lie will allow them to meet their goals. Or it will keep people thinking about you in a certain way. What does any of this matter? Is it reasonable to help others to be happy if all this does is make you unhappy? Does it make sense to help others meet their goals if this defies your own? What is the point in having people think about you in a certain way if that is not really what you believe and what you stand for?

Does it help you if your life has turned into a big lie? To masquerade as something that you are not? To pretend that you enjoy your life and care about what you are doing, and want to succeed when deep down you do not care, you are tired, and want to escape?

Of course not.

You must uncover all of the lies, the baggage, and the falseness in your life, to reveal who you are. We want to shine a light on the precious parts of you that are the actual you.

Imagine if Michelangelo were brought back to life, and he was making a sculpture of your spirit. What parts could he chisel away, because they aren't necessary, they aren't you?

Dig deeper into yourself. What is holding you back?

Are you allowing someone to have power over you, to influence you so much that you are scared of how they will react, of what they will do? What is the point in this if it just takes you further and further from being your true self?

In the end, the problem may not stem from anyone else. It may be yourself. Reflect and consider: What is your role in holding yourself back?

I wonder: are you living out someone else's dream life or your own?

What stops you from being your true self, from living life in your way, from finding your path worth exploring and living? What is the barrier that is preventing you from being who you are? Is there a real barrier? Is it just in your mind?

In the end, are they all just excuses? Are you allowing the barriers to form walls around yourself, stopping your true self from shining through? Are they that powerful?

Have you willingly walked into a prison that has shackled your heart and spirit?

Are you afraid to uncover yourself? Are you so used to being told who you are that you are scared to learn who you actually are and to have to take responsibility for determining your life's path?

Is it a better alternative to hide, deny yourself, and live out someone else's truth rather than pursue your own? Is that really best?

What or who is holding you back?

Is it a person? A thing? A belief? A desire? A habit you do without even thinking? Is it fear or worry? Is it a circumstance or situation that you are in? An event that happened in the past that you can't move beyond?

Lift these boulders off from your legs with all of your might and free yourself.

Ultimately, you may find that you are your own greatest obstacle. You may be the one holding yourself back from being your true self.

This could be because you have developed counterproductive mindsets, habits, and beliefs. Or it may be because of certain people that you have allowed into your life.

You must pinpoint what is holding you back so that you can have an epiphany. This awakening can finally help you to move beyond this and overcome the barriers of your life.

Think back to your old self. Who did you used to be? Was that closer to the real you? Or are you closer to the real you now?

You may find that in having remembered yourself, all you did was stir up old memories. But who you were back then is no longer who you are now. Perhaps back then, you were naïve, more hopeful, more ambitious, or had different interests or beliefs. Now, you have changed, evolved, and you are no longer the same person. This is fine—none of us are the same as we once were.

By now, you may have attempted to uncover yourself. You have found some of what was holding you back, but ultimately you cannot overcome those obstacles so easily. Perhaps you have been working for a boss for 15 years in an industry that you can't stand. You are too far in your career, and to quit now would be irresponsible. Your family relies on your income, and you do not have a backup plan. In such a case, there is no obvious solution. Still, I always remember that the first step toward resolving a problem is in acknowledging that it exists. If you are unsatisfied with your whole life's direction, then this is a truth that you need to explore, and you must consider your options. Your truth is worth fighting for, and you should not simply sit back and live out the most convenient life in front of you.

Is life something that will just happen to you? Or will you rise and let your inner truth shine a light on your life's path?

At this stage, you may have denied your true self for so long that it has become a bad habit. Perhaps this is just your way of life. It is easier to forget about your true self and deny it than to work on discovering it. At least, in the short term, it feels that way. In the long term, you will thank yourself for having pursued your truth wholeheartedly. There is no other way to live. How can it be acceptable to live a lie? It isn't. We must seek our truth.

Your truth is your life. Go for it.

Uncover Yourself

1. Do you feel a weight holding you down, muffling your true self? What can you do about this?
2. Are you spending most of your time on someone else's truth rather than on your own? Can you do something to change this?
3. Is there something about yourself that you miss? Is there a particular quality, talent, value, or personality trait you used to have that got covered up somehow?
4. Have you run away from yourself for so long that you do not know how to find it? Could this mean that you should spend more time nourishing and cultivating your true self?
5. Are you afraid of uncovering your true self? Do you think some parts of you should stay hidden and covered?

Tip: If your ... your own, it can ... help overcome your ...

Action: **Today, think about something in your life that interferes with your ability to be your true self.**

What is pinning you down in the earthquake scenario, making you feel as if you can't move and just be who you are?

Is it a boss who always demands that you do things his way, rather than considering your viewpoint? Does someone in your life often make you feel bad about yourself? Have you lost something of great value, and there is no way to get it back, and you simply have to adapt to this new reality? Perhaps you feel like a failure in some part of your life, which affects your self-esteem or your motivation to try something new.

Get a clear picture of the boulder in your life that is weighing you down.

Then, think of something you can do to remedy this. If a person is covering up your true self, can you talk to this person more openly about your concerns? And if not, can you see this person less and instead focus on other positive relationships? If your self-esteem feels ruined, is there a way you can get some small wins to help gain confidence?

Figure out something you can do to uncover yourself, and take action on it today.

Reason: To find our truth, we must acknowledge when something is holding us back and keeping us from being our true selves. Sometimes, these ~~cles~~ can pile up if we continue to ignore them.

~~problems~~ are deep enough and you cannot make progress on ~~help~~ to pursue a psychologist, therapist, or life coach to ~~problems~~ and strive to live more of your truth.

Recover Yourself

"We are all damaged. We have all been hurt.
We have all had to learn painful lessons. We are
all recovering from some mistake, loss, betrayal,
abuse, injustice or misfortune. All of life is a process
of recovery that never ends. We each must find
ways to accept and move through the pain and
to pick ourselves back up. For each pang of grief,
depression, doubt or despair there is an inverse
toward renewal coming to you in time. Each
tragedy is an announcement that some good will
indeed come in time. Be patient with yourself."

— Bryant McGill, *Simple Reminders*

Part of your journey toward finding yourself and your truth will likely involve recovering parts of yourself. Let's consider a few possible situations.

Perhaps you used to be curious, and you lost that along the way. How can you recover this? Did someone teach you that it was bad or wrong to ask questions or punish you for your curiosity? Can you tell yourself that it is alright to be curious? That it is okay to be yourself, just as you are?

Perhaps you used to be friendly with most people, even strangers, and then something happened. Someone took advantage of your kindness. They took you for granted or expected you to put them first. Maybe sometimes you found yourself giving too much and not getting anything in return. But is being friendly in your core nature? Is there a way to get back to this without allowing others to take advantage?

As another example, did you enjoy being creative, such as writing stories or perhaps drawing? Then you had to grow up and focus on your work, your family, and doing the things that needed to be done. Through time, you made less and less time to express yourself creatively. After a while, you began to fear that you lost any creative talent you may have once had. Perhaps you did try to get creative again, and you had a block in you. You couldn't access that part of yourself so easily anymore. Is there a way to rekindle that creative spirit you always had inside of you?

Ask yourself: What did you used to be, that you aren't anymore, that you wish you still were? Is there a way for you to get that back?

I am not talking about nostalgia—I am not talking about reliving your past. You may sometimes feel like revisiting old photos or memories or talking about those times. That is okay, but here, we are focused on actually recovering something that was lost. Consider what you have lost in yourself that you would like to have once again. This could be some quality about yourself—an interest, a personality characteristic, or an exceptional talent.

Think about it. Whatever you think you lost in yourself has always been there. You can't lose yourself, at least not permanently. You are always there, even if hidden inside of your external self.

Perhaps there is a deeper self, inside of yourself, underneath an outer covering, a shell if you will, and that is the real you.

Again, what are the parts of you that have been hidden, forgotten, or even lost? Wouldn't you like to find those once more?

Keep in mind that you do not need to express some old interest, desire, or quality in the same way that you used to. Perhaps you used to be bold and daring, which got you into harmful and difficult circumstances in your past. That does not mean that being bold and daring is a terrible thing. If these are qualities that are true to yourself, you may look for more appropriate and positive ways to live out these qualities.

Being bold and daring doesn't mean you must get into drugs and gambling. It could mean standing up for yourself and others who need help. It could mean creating groundbreaking works of art. It could involve challenging people in your life to do better. Otherwise, it could entail allowing yourself to be spontaneous and change plans, not needing to do what is expected at all times.

When looking for something in yourself to recover, you may struggle at first. This is because we tend to shield ourselves mentally to protect ourselves from the challenges we face.

But think back—did anyone ever teach you that your way of being was wrong? Did anyone ever show you that your natural tendencies were unacceptable? This type of thing goes back to our childhood. A girl may be told she isn't supposed to play with trucks but with dolls. A boy may be told to toughen up if he gets emotional. If you expressed an interest in doing something, and no one helped you with that interest, perhaps you learned that your desires were not so important. Did you try to speak up about something, but no one cared? Did people make comments about your hair, the way you dressed, the way you talked or walked?

Surely at some point, someone taught you that something about yourself was not right and that you needed to change it. This may have come from a parent, a teacher, a sibling, a friend, or someone else. They may have meant well, but perhaps they were wrong.

Some of the things that happened to us as children do not apply to us as adults, of course. If you wanted to play with a toy, and someone told you that it was for younger children or kids of another gender, then this probably does not meaningfully impact your life anymore. But these experiences can still affect us on a deeper level, as we may learn that we are not fine the way we are—coming to believe that we need to change for someone else.

When people do this to young ones, I would call these "corrective nudges." Whether people mean to or not, they sometimes direct you toward being something different than yourself. In some cases, you are learning to improve and become better. But in other cases, what you are taught may be arbitrary, judgmental, or wrong.

As adults, or as a society in general, we think that we know better. So we guide children to becoming this or that. But what if a child was guided too strongly, and this took him away from becoming himself? Wouldn't that be a tragedy?

Perhaps a child was raised to be a citizen of the world, according to what was generally expected. But is this what is best? Shouldn't we raise that child to be the best version of herself? And doesn't this best version imply to be herself, rather than programmed to be what society wants her to be?

What were you guided toward that was not You? Is there a way to undo this, to get back to being you? To recover the parts of yourself that were once lost?

One way to accomplish this is to find the people who allow you to be yourself the most.

When I think back to high school, I was very introverted. I worried too much about what other people thought or did, like many high schoolers. But with my close group of friends, I felt free to be myself. Sure, I wanted them to like me, but we became good friends because we liked and accepted each other for who we were.

One friend would tell strange and unexpected jokes. He was willing to make people uncomfortable, not caring if someone may take offense. Another would plan out things to do on the weekends, but he would take it personally if anyone made other plans. One of my best friends was my study partner for exams, but he was so competitive when it came to sports or games that playing with him could become a nuisance. I was the studious one, and perhaps I sometimes annoyed my friends for not being fun enough. But we were all friends—at liberty to be ourselves with each other, even when we sometimes felt confined in other parts of our lives.

I wasn't choosing my friends as much as I was simply attracted to becoming friends with the people who allowed me to be myself. They allowed me to be my most truthful self—I didn't have to pretend to be anything else with them.

Think about what circumstances allow you to be yourself the most. What settings? Is it at home, school, work, or with nature? With which people? Is it when you are with family, friends, at church, or even an online community?

Instead of just people, it is also helpful to consider activities that bring out your true self.

With which activities are you able to lose yourself completely in the task? Is it when you're reading, playing an instrument, writing, observing, thinking, problem-solving, giving advice, traveling? What is it? When you *lose yourself* completely in something, and this is a pattern, this means that you are *finding yourself* in that activity. It means that you are in flow, entirely focused, and dedicated. Instead of being you, you become what you are doing because what you do is your most authentic form of expression. Some people search all their lives for that feeling, but perhaps you have already found it in some meaningful task in your own life. If you have, don't lose it.

Become it.

And if you have lost a critical part of yourself, remember that you can always recover it.

KEY QUESTIONS

Recover Yourself

1. When you were younger, do you remember any "corrective nudges" that someone gave you? Perhaps they directed you toward dressing, acting, or speaking differently. How did this affect you?

2. Have you lost a part of yourself that you would like to recover? Is it your creative, reading, optimistic, spontaneous, or friendly self? How can you get started?

3. If you lost a part of yourself along the way, why or how did this happen? Can you stay connected to yourself and avoid having this happen again?

4. Are you nostalgic or longing for something or someone? Do you miss who you were when you had a different lifestyle or person in your life? Is there a way to recover this, or is this just a reality that you must make peace with?

5. What people, group, or place helps you reconnect with who you are and recover your true self? Who do you feel at ease with, where there is no need to put up a front or guard yourself in any way?

TAKE ACTION TODAY

Recover Yourself

Action: **Today, I want you to think of something you would like to recover in your life.** Is it happiness, an old friendship, or a hobby you used to care deeply about? What is something that, if you recovered it, it would mean a lot to you? You wouldn't just be engaging in a task or something that you used to do. You would be recovering a part of yourself.

If you cannot recover this thing that was lost, perhaps you can find something new to take its place. And if nothing can take its place, then it may still help to find something new and positive to introduce into your life.

When you have something in mind you want to recover, take action that will help you to regain this in your life.

Reason: Recovering yourself can sometimes be intimidating. But to make any progress, you have to take action. You have to aim to regain the parts of yourself that have gradually been slipping away.

Tip: If you ever went through a period where you didn't feel like yourself, where you thought you could be depressed, or when you felt like you truly did not belong, that may have been the start of a period where you lost a part of yourself. But there is nothing to worry about. You can choose to regain this back in your life.

Discover Yourself

"Everybody is in a hurry to decode you in a certain way, and then they expect you to adhere to their definition. How can they possibly do that when you yourself are finding it hard to discover yourself?"

— Sushant Singh Rajput

What I will encourage you to do next is look for ways to discover your true self. This means that you should push the boundaries, even if slightly, to illuminate who you are. You may have defined yourself in a certain way, but perhaps those definitions are false or too limited. Maybe you did not explore certain sides of yourself, and so you were not aware that they existed and that they needed to be nurtured as well.

When it comes to different sides of yourself, such as interests, feelings, desires, and so on, simply ask yourself: "Did I give it a chance?" When you can, aim to say "yes" to more. If you are invited to an event and are not convinced that you will like it, go anyway. Go to new places. Explore new kinds of music. When you are inclined to do something, allow yourself to try it, even if it costs a bit of money or takes some extra time to work on. The experiences and relationships you build are worth more than the bit of cash or time spent.

This world is infinitely rich in what it allows us to do. Most importantly, everyone and everything around us is a chance to learn about ourselves more deeply. And as already discussed, *We Must Know Ourselves Before We Can Know Anything Else.*

Understand that you can only remember, uncover, and recover so much of yourself. But when you discover, the opportunities are limitless. There is always a new side of yourself to explore that you did not know was even there.

Keep in mind that you are likely mistaken if you think you know all there is to know about yourself. Just as the universe is rich and complex, and there is always more to explore, this also applies to yourself.

The difference is that we can easily find 100 books on virtually any topic, with a bit of research. But there is no book about you. Unless, of course, there happens to be a biography about you. But even if there is a biography written about you, how deeply can it truly explore you? The odds are that it would explore your actions or a few different aspects of your life. But in theory, tens or hundreds of volumes could have been written about any individual on the planet.

The volumes could contain self-reflections, world views, beliefs, lessons learned, emotions, people who influenced you, critical events and situations, interests, and thoughts. I am envisioning all of these subjects as being split up into separate volumes. Yet, in reality, you could explore yourself more deeply by intermixing all of these topics. For example, your thoughts will influence your emotions, which affect your behaviors. Your upbringing and your parents influence your beliefs and desires. Every aspect of yourself influences every other part of yourself. They are not all disassociated and disconnected—instead, they are integrated and interconnected.

How many volumes would need to be filled to capture who you are?

The more you explore yourself and the world and focus on discovering your true self, the more whole and complete, one with yourself, and

interconnected you will feel. You will feel congruent, in harmon
out a truth that will be manifested in all areas of your life.

As a part of discovering your truth, you may at times take actions that you regret. Regret is a powerful way to find truth because regret is just telling you that you walked a path of falseness, and it is urging you to learn from this.

Ultimately, regret is just a feeling that originates from your self. You will learn that *this is bad. Do not do this again. Do something different next time.*

If you think of it, regret is just pointing out that you made a mistake. But I always like to say, "there are no mistakes." Every mistake you make just shines a light on what you should be doing and helps you move away from what you should not be doing. Mistakes help you to learn, grow, and evolve.

As a way of finding your true self, it can be perfectly reasonable to do more, make more mistakes, and open yourself up to new ways of being. Counter to what you may expect, making mistakes on purpose (avoiding catastrophic ones, of course) can be a perfectly reasonable way to learn and grow.

If you struggle to push yourself into new ways of being and seeing, find someone who can help you along. This may be someone adventurous who enjoys travel or is curious about new and stimulating thoughts. Or it may be someone who wants to help you learn about yourself more deeply.

Remember the aim here. It isn't just to do new stuff for the sake of doing it. The objective is to explore new parts of yourself and hopefully to discover something.

Keep in mind that some people may not need to do new things to discover themselves. They may not need to thrust themselves into the world, look-ing for new activities, interests, books, and ways of seeing.

Instead, some people may find that they have much of the truth deep inside, and they just need to explore it further and discover it for themselves.

Understand that just as deep and complex as the universe is, that your mind itself is also profound and complex. Think of it. The universe is infinitely complex, and your mind is not capable of grasping all of it. Yet, the fact that you can conceptualize what this universe is in any way is a magnificent feat.

Your **mental universe** *or mind must be quite an advanced system* to process the universe we live in. I am convinced that our inner world and life are magnitudes more rich and complex than most of us know them to be. Those who don't think so may just not have explored their mental universe deeply enough.

As a way of finding your truth, you may choose to forget about the world and universe for a moment and instead decide to explore your inner life. As I said, there are volumes upon volumes worth of books that could be written on all of us. Explore your inner self and truth, and you may find yourself writing some of those volumes in the form of a journal or even a book.

How exactly can you explore your mental universe? I believe the trick to doing this is spending time alone, with your thoughts and feelings, and aiming to explore them more deeply. It's not enough to randomly sift through them. You must consciously explore them, looking for patterns, meaning, truth, purpose, and your true self inside of yourself. Perhaps this truth is hidden, and you must go on a treasure hunt for it.

You can go on a journey of self-discovery just by exploring your mind. Run through situations you have been in. How did you handle them? What could you have done better? Did you manage them in a way that was true to yourself?

Sit alone with yourself and ask:

- What are the central questions of my life that I should be
- Why am I always unhappy, anxious, or impatient?
- What was the biggest mistake of my life?
- What can I do today to improve the way I feel about my life?
- Am I stuck? Why is that? Can I get unstuck?
- Is there someone who can help me to find my truth?
- Is there a pattern of problems that follow me no matter where I go or what I do? Why is that?

The value of spending time alone is learning not to be distracted by the chatter of other voices. Your next step will be to learn to quiet the voices in your mind, to achieve true silence. This will help you to pursue the truth that is already within you.

To make progress with quieting your surroundings and your mind, I recommend meditation. You don't need to force yourself to think about anything. Instead, relax yourself and your mind, and observe the thoughts that pop up. Imagine being in a bubble bath, and bubbles float up, and in those bubbles are your thoughts. You can see them, explore them, and decide whether they are helping or hurting you. You do not need to absorb them and internalize them, necessarily.

Usually, meditation is done with thoughts in mind, but you can meditate any way you like. You can focus on feelings instead. As you think about certain things, what feelings come up? What does that mean? Why do you feel so strongly about certain people or events? Are these feelings helping or hurting you?

What about desires? If any desires come up, what are they about? Are some of these desires and wishes you have had your whole life? Why do you want them so badly? Have you worked hard at them or just viewed them as a dream that was not worth pursuing wholeheartedly? Have these desires motivated you to improve yourself? Or have they made you feel unworthy?

What about relationships? If you think of some relationships in your life, how are they going? What role are you playing? What role is the other person playing? Are these loving or positive bonds based on trust, or are they based on competition or ill-will of some kind? Which relationships are worth working on, and which are not? Are these relationships growing into something worthwhile or disintegrating with time?

In meditation, you can reflect on your thoughts and feelings. You can observe yourself. Then you can ask: "Am I the person experiencing these thoughts and feelings, or am I the one who is observing them and consciously choosing the effect that they will have on my life?"

You can meditate on anything you wish. You can explore your life from many different angles, going deeper and deeper into who you are, why you are the way you are, where you want to be, and what you are doing to get there.

Asking questions is critical because you can find deeper ways to explore and discover something new about yourself.

At this point, you have learned some valuable techniques to help pursue your truth. We have discussed how you can remember, uncover, recover, and discover yourself. Now, all that is left is to create yourself. We will explore this idea in the next chapter.

KEY QUESTIONS

Discover Yourself

1. Do you shy away from new experiences, or have you been viewing them as an opportunity to discover new parts of yourself?

2. How often do you discover something new about yourself? Do you feel that you have been the same for the past five years, or has something changed about you?

3. Is there some part of yourself you have ignored that may be worth exploring? Is there something you always wanted to do or try that you neglected?

4. How often do you spend time alone, at peace with yourself? Does the idea of doing this make you uncomfortable, and why is that?

5. Have your dreams pointed you toward something that you may want to discover in yourself? Sometimes, our dreams indicate something we are longing for, that we have denied ourselves.

TAKE ACTION TODAY

Discover Yourself

Action: **Today, the next time you would normally say "No," consider saying "Yes" this time.** For example, maybe someone will ask you for a favor. Or perhaps someone will invite you to a gala or party that you would typically not consider attending.

Another way to apply today's action is to pay more attention to your thoughts. Perhaps you are browsing clothes at a store, and your first thought is, "No—that is not my style." Instead, consider that you might like this article of clothing if only you were to try it on.

Pay close attention when your mind says "No," and take just an extra moment to consider if you might discover something new about yourself by saying "Yes."

Reason: When we avoid doing new things, we can become too comfortable and more closed off. In time, we may decide that we will avoid any experience if we don't expect to enjoy it. But that mindset prevents us from discovering the boundaries of our true self.

Tip: I used to struggle with doing new things, so I know what it is like. Perhaps you are apprehensive about jumping into something new. In that case, my advice is to start small. For example, if large gatherings make you uncomfortable, then make an effort to meet up in a smaller group. Or, if unpredictable environments make you uncomfortable, ask for additional information before committing to a particular activity. The point is to make an effort. Dare to do something new, even if you usually would not have done it.

Create Yourself

"Trust yourself. Create the kind of self that you will be happy to live with all your life. Make the most of yourself by fanning the tiny, inner sparks of possibility into flames of achievement."

— Golda Meir

Ask yourself: What is lacking in my life, which I would like to have? What is something I have never had in the way I wanted? And is this something that I have the power to will into existence?

To get glimpses into what this may be, look at what you have surrounded yourself with. Do you have outgoing and spontaneous friends, while you are more introverted and methodical, or vice versa? Do you look up to people who have certain qualities? Perhaps they are confident and witty, and you don't think you possess these qualities.

Otherwise, think about anything you have ever envied. Are you jealous of some people for what they have been able to accomplish? Rather than wasting your energy on jealousy, why not plan to become more like them if that is what you truly want.

Consider: Are there some qualities, skills, or abilities you want, which have always seemed out of reach?

Before going much further, ask yourself if this need or desire is coming from your true self. Is this something that you want to become because it is already a part of you? Keep in mind that some qualities are not a natural part of us, but we can learn, grow, and become them if we make an effort.

I am talking about something here that is often ignored. I am talking about creating yourself and building yourself into what you want to be. If you do not have a self you are happy with, or proud of, or comfortable with, then create that version of yourself.

You have probably heard of stories where someone was bullied or even beaten up as a child. Hence, they decide to become a bodybuilder or to learn karate. This is admirable—they have decided to create who they needed to be to meet their goals. They did not want to be a target that was harassed and had no self-confidence. Instead of being a victim, they flipped the script and became the hero of their own story. This is a classic example of how we can create ourselves, despite our faults or unfortunate life experiences.

Many of us fail to understand that we can do this along any of our human dimensions. Not as smart as you would like to be? There is a path to get there. I have written many books that could help with this—for example, *The Secret Principles of Genius*. This isn't easy. A bodybuilder will train every day, lifting weights to work different sets of muscles, and eat a diet to help meet specific goals, constantly measuring progress. Why would the necessary work be any different for building your intellect?

I am aware that many people will argue that the intellect cannot be increased. To me, the argument is not important. You can learn strategies that will improve your thinking and problem-solving, and by doing this, you can improve the results in your life in a wide range of areas. If you can think smarter and take more intelligent actions, then practically speaking, you have increased your intellectual abilities.

One of the greatest mistakes we make is assuming we cannot improve in critical areas of our lives.

For a long time, I had a fear of public speaking. I assumed that this could not be fixed and that I was a hopeless case. When I was accepted into graduate school in 2009, I realized that public speaking would be a way of life there. I needed to learn to manage this fear and overcome it. The only other option was to run away from it. And running away did cross my mind. I figured: *I could just drop out of the program before it even began. I could change careers.* And then I realized how silly I was being. Was I going to reroute my entire life's plan just because of a simple fear?

Keep in mind that as a child, I was a student who dreaded presentations so much that I began skipping school for this reason. I was an excellent student, but my Achilles' heel was needing to speak for a few minutes in front of a crowd. I had my rituals the night before such assignments. One time, I prayed for a foot of snow, another time for the teacher to forget to call my name to deliver the presentation. Another time, I prayed to get just sick enough to be excused from the assignment, and then I would quickly recover. It's amusing to me now that even in my total dread of public speaking, I hadn't considered the idea that I could pray to overcome my fear of it. Somehow, that seemed too farfetched.

I am the person who considered for a minute giving up on graduate school before even beginning. I did go, in the end. And as I predicted, I was expected to deliver presentations frequently. At the end of my first year, I had my biggest one. I presented my research to over 100 people. It went very well. All I did was stop focusing on the fear and worry. Instead, I redirected my attention to helping others, to educate them. Every presentation is about teaching someone something, so that was what I chose to focus on. This change in mindset allowed me to overcome my fear.

When I got over the fear of speaking to crowds, I thought: *Maybe we can improve at anything. Maybe IQs can go up if we just work at it. Perhaps any fear can be overcome. If you set a goal to improve in some area of your life, you can eventually get there.*

I would like you to note that this is a pattern I have rediscovered in my life so many times, in so many different areas. I often thought: *I can't do this. I'm not good enough. I don't know where to start.* Then I would end up doing it. In time, I would barely recognize myself. I was no longer the person who was scared to speak to others. I was no longer the person whose memory was not good enough (as discussed in *Practical Memory)* or mentally healthy enough (as discussed in *7 Thoughts to Live Your Life By).*

I became a new me because I had created myself in this way.

This is such an important topic that I want this point to hit home for you. Whatever it is you want to create in yourself, you can get there. It may not be easy, and you may need some help, but you can do it. But you can't go in halfheartedly. You have to go in with all your heart. Then, things tend to fall into place.

Something I have never mentioned to a soul out of shame, but which I would like to share with you is that a psychologist once diagnosed me with a "Disorder of written expression," a learning disability that I didn't even know existed. I became aware of this diagnosis when I was in graduate school, at the time in my life when I was struggling the most. I had already been diagnosed with major depressive disorder and dysthymia, but this was the last thing I expected to get diagnosed with.

I had never been worried about my writing ability or been informed by any teacher that I may have problems with writing. Yet, a psychologist diagnosed me with this. Then she explained that I would suffer great difficulties in keeping up with the standard of writing expected.

And in my career path, the standards of writing were high. In the graduate program, I was expected to write and publish academic articles regularly. I needed to be able to self-edit my writing. If word got out that I had this disorder, I felt that I would be a laughingstock.

I was upset for a few days about it, and then I threw her analysis in the trash. I decided to forget about it (until now.)

A label can dictate your life if you let it. Even when I was in graduate school, writing was a passion of mine. I wanted to be a professional writer, even back then.

And so it left me with a horrible feeling, to think for even a moment that perhaps I would not be able to make it in a career that involved writing. The self-doubt was beginning, which was why I threw away the analysis and diagnosis—to help release its hold on me.

When I threw it away, it felt like a magic spell had been broken. I would not let this label set a limit on my abilities.

Unfortunately, we tend to set limits on ourselves. If you are lucky enough to have avoided that up to now, someone else may be tempted to impose them on you. We must overcome that restrictive part of our nature. We must tap into our limitless abilities, our ability to create ourselves as we envision or desire ourselves to be.

You can improve leaps and bounds beyond what you imagined possible. Why sell yourself short? Why set limitations on yourself that are not actually there?

Virtually anything can be trained or strengthened. The question is whether you know the path to get there, whether you have the right resources and training available to you, and whether you have a strong enough will to accomplish this. Here are some qualities that could be trained: intellect, empathy, intuition, communication skills, problem-solving, creativity, leadership, computer skills, foreign languages, self-defense, survival skills, a positive mindset, the ability to make friends, networking, writing, self-awareness, and spirituality. This is just a sampling of the possibilities.

For every topic, there are books, courses, videos, podcasts, blogs, articles, coaches, and therapists who can help you if you just take a moment to look up the information.

Creating yourself has never been easier. The information is all out there, but it is still hard work. Just because it is there doesn't mean the path is easy.

The fundamental question is: What is worth spending time on to improve from my core, from the inside to the outside?

Explore any disappointments in your life. What are your regrets? What are some excuses that you often make to cover up something that you dislike about yourself? Is there any shame you have carried with you, where perhaps you are too ashamed to even speak of it? Is there a hole in your spirit that is holding you back? Look at these sore spots in your life, and shine a light on them, at least for yourself to see them more clearly. If you are in denial about who you are, it will be difficult to make progress.

Look at yourself as a scientific specimen. People give their bodies to science. You should donate your mind to an objective self-exploration. This means that you can see yourself from afar, not as yourself, but as someone else might see you. You can examine yourself and your mind from a distant land and see yourself for *what* you are. This is a safe space where you do not need to hide anything. You can display your flaws, fears, and secret shames for all that they are because no one will try to use them against you or judge you for it.

Your objective and detached self is here in the role of a doctor, therapist, or shaman to help make you better again. Maybe there is nothing wrong with you at all. Perhaps all you need is to be given a chance to find your true self, to live your life.

When you explore your deepest flaws, fears, and shames, you will see that there is a path to create yourself the way you want to be.

Let's consider an example.

Perhaps when you get into new relationships, you tend to think that you will not be good enough for this person. This belief leads you to fear losing them before the relationship even gets started. Then you become too attached to this person too soon, which frightens them away. They don't like it. They want their space. The relationship ends fast, and you feel even worse about yourself. Perhaps you have a cycle like this. Maybe not this one, but another one where your flaws, fears, and shames create the same vicious cycle for you, again and again. Think about them. What are the vicious cycles of your life?

Can you create yourself so that you can overcome this?

Can you NOT be limited by your past, and somehow overcome all of it, and transcend it?

In the above case, rather than faking confidence, could you dig deeper and build confidence within you to overcome your constant relationship troubles? Is your lack of confidence because you are not as educated or skilled as your friends? Could you seek out that education? Or if going to university seems out of reach, can you at least acquire some valuable skills so that you can create the life you have always wanted for yourself? Would that give you the confidence to not always be worried about losing the person you have only just begun dating?

Search for the vicious patterns of your life. What are they? Do you often procrastinate? This is usually a signal that you are resisting something. You don't really want to do this task, so you leave it until the last possible moment, and then it fails horribly. Because it fails horribly, you become convinced that you are unskilled, not smart enough, and not good enough. Yet, in reality, you sabotaged yourself. Even if you tend to procrastinate and still succeed at your goals, in the end, this is a sign that you do not honestly want to be on the path that you are on. In that case, is there something you can change to guide yourself back to your truth?

Do you allow someone else to have power and control over you? Do you let them have their way because it is easier? Is it a vicious cycle where you do what they say, then you regret having followed the path that they told you to go on? Perhaps you have neglected your true self along the way.

Do you often get into the same type of arguments, where the same problem comes up, again and again? Is there something in who you are as a person that is lacking? Can you create what is needed to fill that void in yourself to overcome this problem?

The first step toward growth is always to become aware that a problem exists. If you are happy and satisfied with everything in your life, there is nothing to fix, nothing that you need to create in yourself.

But this is a book about truth, after all. So I would encourage you to *dig deeper*. Don't lie to yourself, just because it is convenient to pretend as if everything is fine. If you don't have any significant problems, that is great. But if you have substantial issues holding you back, you must acknowledge them, confront them, and work on them. This is the path forward.

The last thing you need to do is look for an easy path. The easy route is usually not the most truthful one. Dig deep inside and look for anything you are not truly happy with about yourself.

Do you often try to cover up something about yourself, so others will not notice it? What is it? Why do you do that? Do you make light of certain topics for others to think that you don't care when it matters to you a lot? Do you wear a mask in public to make it seem as if everything is going well, then at home, you collapse in a depression, in exhaustion, or over-whelmed with anxiety?

Perhaps you value self-sufficiency. Do you sometimes try to take on too much all on your own? You may refuse to ask for help no matter what. This stubbornness results in failures, and then you feel terrible about your inability to thrive.

Look deeply into yourself to discover what is worth adding to your life. Think it through carefully because developing qualities and building skills will take great dedication. To do this right will take time and effort. You may be tempted to give up at times. Only you can decide if something is important enough that it is worth investing yourself into it.

Decide who you need or want to be. Decide the person you want to create in yourself, then do it wholeheartedly, and never look back.

To do this successfully, you should have a larger purpose in mind. Perhaps if you have been bullied, you will learn karate to protect yourself at first. But in time, you may wish to help protect your family or the people around you as well. Ask yourself if there is a larger purpose here beyond just yourself. This will motivate you to keep going even during difficult times.

I would caution you against creating something in yourself just because it is trendy and others do it. Do not take creating and building yourself lightly.

This will be an epic, deep, spiritual, and creative quest to make yourself into who you want and need to be. Don't settle for anything less.

As a final note, in this chapter, I mentioned that I once threw away a psychologist's analysis. If you have received an analysis or diagnosis from your psychologist, I do *not* recommend throwing it away. Speak to your healthcare provider or get a second opinion to learn more about any diagnoses that you may receive. If you need mental healthcare and are not satisfied with your provider, then discuss that with your provider. If necessary, consider switching to another one that can better meet your needs.

KEY QUESTIONS

Create Yourself

1. What are some abilities, skills, or qualities that you always wanted to develop in yourself, but you never did? Is this just because you told yourself a story that you couldn't do it?

2. Is your view of yourself entirely focused on the things that happened to you in your past? Will you allow some room for yourself to create who you want to be?

3. Have you ever tried to look at yourself objectively? Can you see yourself from the perspective of a neutral, unbiased person?

4. What is a problem that you often have in life? What was your role in creating this? Has it become a vicious cycle? What do you need to create in your life to break free from this?

5. Who do you admire the most in this world? What specific qualities, traits, or habits do you like about that person? Could you absorb some of those and make yourself into a person who has those qualities as well?

TAKE ACTION TODAY

Create Yourself

Action: **Think about your deepest issue holding you back in life from being the person you need, want, and deserve to be.** Is it fear? Is it an experience that you were never able to make peace with fully? Is it the lack of a particular skill or ability? Could it even be the lack of self-awareness?

When you have your deepest issue or biggest flaw in mind, **create a list of actions** to improve in that area of your life. Then **select one that you can work on starting today and do it.**

Reason: To create yourself the way that you need, want, and deserve to be, you must first identify a big issue in your life that is holding you back from getting there. There is no shame in admitting this. I have noticed many big problems in my own life. Sometimes, people around me would also point out these flaws. The point is that in acknowledging these issues, you will be able to find a path forward. However, if we are in denial of such problems, it won't be easy to progress.

Tip: If you have trouble figuring out a key issue in your life, send an email to a few close friends and family members and ask them what they think is holding you back. Tell them that you want their complete honesty and openness and that you will not get upset at hearing the truth from them. You may mention that you wish to identify critical issues in your life to overcome them and create a better version of yourself.

Consider some simple but effective ways to improve your life: Are you eating and sleeping well? Are you getting exercise? Are you making time for meditation and mindfulness? Are you treating the people in your life with love and kindness? Are you managing your finances appropriately? Which of these could benefit you the most? Let's work on that.

Know Yourself Deeply

"Don't look at someone else and want to
be them. Search within yourself and find out
who you are and be someone positive."

— Kelly Rowland

I've already discussed the importance of knowing yourself in previous chapters. However, knowing yourself is pivotal to finding your truth, and I find it essential to delve into this even more deeply here. The hope is that with this chapter, you will be able to delve more deeply into yourself.

Something that seems to escape us is that we have a universe inside of us. The mind itself is like its own unique universe, and as I've mentioned, I like to call this the mental universe.

For anything in the universe, you can experience it and perceive it through many dimensions. For example, there are the senses. These include taste, touch, feeling, sight, and smell. You can also experience emotions—such as love, happiness, pride, shame, and fear. Of course, often, for the things we perceive and sense, we build associations between them. So for anything in the universe, you can consider how it relates to everything else you know.

There are also many ways of understanding. For example, do you know the process of how something works? Do you know its purpose? Are you familiar with the inputs and outputs of that process? Then there is imagination. For anything you experience, you could use that to come up with creative ideas.

Also, consider that for anything we explore in the universe, we are exploring a part of our minds. Anything that we sense in the universe is ultimately experienced as patterns of neurons firing in the brain. We do not get the direct experience of anything. Instead, we have the experience of having an experience. To have direct experience would mean to be something. However, the only thing that we get to be is ourselves.

We have the direct experience of being ourselves.

And having that experience means that we experience the universe through our selves (e.g., our mind, senses, and feelings). Since we are a part of the universe, our human experience is just one small part of the universe, experiencing another much larger part of the universe.

All our lives, we explore the universe around us. We have thoughts about everything happening around us. And often, the thoughts we have about ourselves may just be us absorbing ideas from the people around us. If someone says we are selfish, then we believe it. If they say we are spontaneous, then we come to think so. Whatever it is that they say, we may come to agree with it.

Most of our senses and ways of knowing are there to help us gather information about the world. However, some senses help us understand ourselves, such as self-reflection and our sense of temperature, balance, and pain or pressure.

The only sense we have that truly helps us learn about ourselves, in terms of our truth and who we are, is self-reflection. Some of us may struggle with self-reflection for a variety of reasons. It can seem boring, selfish, or even pointless. But these are superficial thoughts, and we should dig deeper.

For every aspect of the universe, we have our inner way of processing it. Consider that the universe has multiple dimensions—length, height, width, the space-time continuum, and then perhaps even deeper dimensions that we cannot perceive.

We also have our experience-based dimensions from which we can process the universe itself. As already stated, there are our physical senses, and then there are emotion, understanding, and imagination. Rather than physical dimensions, these may be our four basic dimensions of experience. And there are likely many deeper ones that we are not fully aware of, from which we can experience the universe.

The point of this section is to help you have this realization—just as complex and deep as the whole universe may be, so is your mind, inner experience, and your truth. Your inner experiences may be much richer and more complex than you think they are. This is why I refer to them as the mental universe.

Just as there are hidden aspects of the universe that are unknown to you, there are also hidden aspects of your mind that you have not yet explored.

I'm not convinced that most of us know that much about ourselves. We do not explore our minds and truths very deeply. We are taught to look at the world but not to look into ourselves.

We may know a few dimensions of ourselves well. Perhaps you know what your interests are, but why are these your interests? For everything that you are and that you do, there is a WHY behind it. Why are you that way? WHO is your **TRUE SELF**?

Let me tell you about my friend James.

James was always drawn to music. He always enjoyed music and wanted to play it, and so he learned to play the trumpet from a young age. He was phenomenal at it, but why was the music so important to him? Well, it made him feel good. It melted away the pains in his life and gave him something to look forward to. As an adult, he became a music teacher because he wanted to help students build up this feeling. For anyone who was struggling in life, he wanted them to have something to look forward to, so they could experience the joys of making music.

But why did their feelings matter so much to him? James saw himself in his music students—often, the kids he worked with had troubles and pains of their own, and he was attuned to that. He could relate to their daily challenges.

But why did James get into music specifically? Sure, he was always drawn to it, but why? Well, he had an uncle who played the trumpet wonderfully. He was always fascinated by the spirit of the sound he was able to produce.

So there we have it. Maybe we are just drawn to certain truths and ways of being.

The universe is pulling us in specific directions, and we get to choose whether to flow along with it, resist it, or deny it.

But there is something about James that I failed to mention. Let's dig deeper into that.

When James was a child, he heard his parents shouting at each other in his home. They spent years shouting at each other, and he would often feel lonely and empty inside. Finally, his parents decided to divorce. But during all of that shouting, James would practice the trumpet, focusing on developing his musical spirit. This was his way to muffle out the noise and forget about it. Eventually, he learned to crowd out the pains and sorrows of his life with the joys of music.

He played the trumpet before, during, and after his parents' divorce. In time, the trumpet became an extension of his feelings, emotions, even his fingers. He and the trumpet were in sync.

Now, James is someone who knows who he is. He is the trumpet.

The above analysis is succinctly put, but it took an ongoing dialogue between James and me to understand who James was, deep inside. He has a talent with the trumpet and a way of teaching that skill that no one else seems to have. But we cannot understand James in full until we realize the origins of how he ended up becoming one with the trumpet.

Now I ask: *Who are you? What are you?*

Take some time to explore your inner universe of being more deeply.

What makes you angry, scared, worried, doubtful, resentful, hurt, confused, overwhelmed, or sad?

What makes you happy, ecstatic, amazed, gives you a rush of energy, empowers you, and fulfills you?

Explore your thoughts. How did you used to think about things? Has that changed in time? Are you more positive or negative now? More certain or doubtful? More spontaneous or methodical?

Allow yourself to be alone, to daydream, to have your mind wander, to think about anything you want. Give yourself some time to not have to *do* anything, but just to *be*.

Then, consider: What is it you hope to get out of life?

How have you shifted through the years? Are you mostly the same, or have you changed in some meaningful way?

What parts of you are the same, and what parts are different?

It's normal for some parts of you to stay the same through the years and for others to gradually shift. Even the parts of you that stay the same may become more refined or adapt in some way.

We can't stay the same, as we are constantly responding to our environment. Any minor change in your situation or environment may alter how you react and respond to it.

Imagine digging deeper and deeper into yourself. Visualize a never-ending forest or even a personally created universe of your own. Imagine that it's not the universe we live in, but one that you have personally made up. Conjure this in your mind: You see a tree, and it looks beautiful. This is your truth. You see a squirrel looking for food. This is your truth. You see someone crying, and you know they are sad. These are all your truths. You know these thoughts to be accurate, but it is just part of your way of experiencing the universe. You made this.

You have to get in tune with that. When you know something to be true, stay with it. Listen to other people and how they see things, but always keep in mind your natural state. Your way of seeing and experiencing is your truth. Don't cast that aside. Stay with it. Remember it. Live it.

When you sense the truth based on your feelings, emotions, intuitions, knowledge, personal experiences, and so on, then this is real. Ultimately, the more ways you experience and know something, the more you can be sure that it is true.

Your truth is ultimately your complete universe. And your universe is just all of the dimensions of your experiences added together. As long as you move toward your true self, living your life as authentically as you can, everything about you is true.

The falseness in our lives is often a temporary thing. To live in falseness, we need to be in complete denial. Unfortunately, we are capable of lying to ourselves for quite an extended period. Eventually, living in the lies can feel comfortable. It's easier to carry on with the lie, even if that lie becomes our whole lives. When everything about your life is a lie, you want to believe it is true. You want to think this is your life, and this is real, solid, and concrete. But it isn't. When you have built up this lie, you may find that you are chasing others' dreams, taking on other people's personalities, doing what they want you to do, and thinking like them. When this happens, we have walked the path of falseness and need to get back on track.

This is like spending your time and energy on building a sandcastle, one that can easily crumble with the wind, exposure to water, or any disturbance at all. Of course, this is to be avoided.

What you can do to find your inner self and explore your inner universe is identify parts of yourself and ask: *Is this me, or did I take this on from someone else? Do I really think this, or am I just an echo, repeating what someone else said?* You have to start asking yourself: *What is the line that separates me from everyone and everything else?*

The reality is that we are all intertwined. You were raised by your parents, which their parents raised, and on and on. Some habits and patterns get passed down, over and over.

In this way, greatness can be passed on. For example, suppose one of the best scientists in the world is in your family. In that case, he may be able to teach you greatness—and maybe he learned it from another scientist in the family.

On the other side, if you have an abusive parent, perhaps they had an abusive parent, and on and on. Then you may be predisposed to becoming abusive, even if that is not truly you.

In the last chapter, we ended on the idea that you get to *Create Yourself.* Here, we should consider that ultimately you get to decide who you are. Who you are is going to involve everything you have ever seen and experienced. So there is a YOU who is attached to everyone and everything around you. And then there is a distinct YOU who is separate. For your purposes, what you need to figure out is **Who You Truly Are**. Some of **The Real You** will involve qualities that you grew up with, but you can also create new parts of yourself that never existed before.

Perhaps everyone in your family is a doctor. Just because they are interested in medicine and helping patients get better does not necessarily mean that this is your calling. Your family may influence your life's path, but ultimately you get to decide which route you will take.

To explore your inner universe will ultimately mean to look into uncharted parts of yourself. As cartographers have mapped out parts of the world that were once unknown, you can look into aspects of yourself that were once unknown to you. Rather than accepting that you are a certain way or have certain habits or strengths and weaknesses, you can begin to question it.

Do you have to be that way?

If someone labeled you in a certain way and you held onto this all of your life—are you really that label? Or has thinking that you were this label just affected you and turned you into it?

Imagine an experiment where a child is told how poorly behaved he is all of the time. Now, imagine that this is a child who tries to do the right thing. Yet, every single time the child does something that is not perfect in this imaginary experiment, everyone is ready to tell him how bad he is. They say to the child he will amount to nothing, that everything he does is wrong, and that he is awful at following the rules.

Eventually, if the adults in this child's life are persistent enough in highlighting all the wrongness of this child, I believe he would grow up to become a criminal. This is because he would internalize the belief that he is rotten, destined to be a complete failure.

Then, is this child's inner essence criminal? No—he was just guided in this direction, and he struggled to release himself from this label. He believed that everything he did was awful, leading to trouble, and he was sucked into that reality.

Someone else wrote his life story, and he just lived it out.

Have you ever allowed someone else to write out a part of your story? Have you ever given them that power?

The wonderful thing is that even if you have done so, it doesn't need to be that way. You can learn about yourself, spend some time getting to know your truth, and take back your power to live your life on your terms.

If you don't like the story someone else has written out for you to live, then write your own.

If your life were a novel and you were sketching out yourself as a character, how would you do it? What type of character have you been? Where are you headed? Is your path headed straight for disaster? Then rewrite the story. Flip the script and change things up—it's not too late to make a U-turn or take a detour in your life!

When you know yourself deeply, you hold power to guide yourself to where you need to go.

KEY QUESTIONS

Know Yourself Deeply

1. Is there someone or something that you rely on to show you the way? Are you giving too much power to an outside force?

2. Do you believe that there is a whole mental universe for you to explore? If so, how does that make you feel? Are you scared, excited, or feeling some other emotion?

3. Can you make time to explore your inner world? To just daydream, write in a journal, meditate, and think about your life, thoughts, beliefs, and purpose?

4. Has anyone ever labeled you, and you felt that you were destined or compelled to live out that label? Have you been able to overcome that?

5. What did you think of the story with James and the trumpet? Do you have a story like this that guided you into becoming who you are now?

TAKE ACTION TODAY

Know Yourself Deeply

French mathematician and philosopher Blaise Pascal said: "All of humanity's problems stem from man's inability to sit quietly in a room alone." I often think of this quote, as I have seen the power of sitting in silence, not expecting or needing anything to happen. This activity will allow you to open up the doorway to see your true self.

Action: **Go into a room alone with as little noise as possible, without disruptions, and sit. That is all.** You don't need to meditate. You don't need to have a plan of action. Just sit there for 10 minutes. If you can do that, try 20 minutes. If you get to this point, then keep going. Keep sitting, longer and longer, going through your process of self-discovery.

Reason: We spend so much time learning about other people, the world, and the universe. It is just as important, if not more, that we take some time to figure out ourselves. This can only be done by self-reflection. We hold the keys to the greatest truths about ourselves, and so we must learn to begin our self-exploratory journeys into the heart, mind, and soul.

Tip: Find a quiet room at a quiet time when you are unlikely to be disturbed. If you would like, you may also pursue a dark room or close your eyes. I recommend sitting up to avoid falling asleep. You can purposely reflect on different periods of your life, or you can allow your mind to wander and see what is running through your mind.

Understand that if you have not made the time to get to know yourself, you may be surprised at what you discover. There may be hurtful memories or thoughts in your mind. Or you may be more creative than you expected and have a flurry of ideas. Perhaps you will feel bored or dissatisfied at first, and that is fine. It can take time to get comfortable with sitting alone with yourself. But it's well worth it.

When You Know Yourself, You Know the Right Way to Be

"To know yourself as the Being underneath the thinker, the stillness underneath the mental noise, the love and joy underneath the pain, is freedom, salvation, enlightenment."

— Eckhart Tolle, *The Power of Now*

When we don't know who we are, and when we don't know our truth, we hesitate, question ourselves, and lack confidence. Then not knowing who we are becomes not knowing what to do.

There is this feeling of being lost that feels heavy on the shoulders. It weighs you down. It makes you wonder if anything is worth doing.

Many people will be easily led astray when they don't know themselves. In such cases, we may be easily guided around by a parent or older sibling. It could feel sensible to do what someone else says when we are not sure of what we truly stand for. However, there is a difference between learning and growing through someone's help versus following their truth blindly. When we have lost ourselves, we may be susceptible to joining a cult in the more extreme cases. This is because we will be starving for meaning, purpose, and identity, where we lack these things for ourselves.

When I was a college student at Purdue University (around 2003-2007), I felt that I needed to work to support myself. So several times, I learned about positions that didn't require any experience. Each time, the job was described only vaguely in the advertisement, and when I showed up for the interview, they caught me by surprise. Instead of being an actual interview, they seemed to have a sales pitch to convince me and a group of candidates to become part of their team. These were salespeople, and they wanted to sell me the idea that selling stuff for them would be good for me.

I felt deceived, as though they purposely kept the job description vague because they knew if they mentioned it was a sales position, fewer people would have been interested. I am, by nature, an introvert and not much of a salesperson. I have always been truthful, and I cannot convince myself that any merchandise or service is essential, so how could I convince someone else?

Back then, I didn't know myself very well. In these sales sessions, I felt lost. Under different circumstances, perhaps I would have joined along, just to try to find a part of myself through the sales position. Yet, a few things that I did know about myself were that I was on the introverted side, I was more of a thinker, and I valued the truth.

For one of these sessions, I felt like I was being indoctrinated to join a cult. I won't mention the company, but in this case, I had no idea what the job would involve, yet I showed up. The interview seemed to be done just as a matter of procedure and for no real purpose. They asked a couple of basic questions, and then they shuffled me to a room where they proceeded to pitch the sales job to me. Many other candidates were present as well.

At that point, I realized that I knew this company's product, as it had a certain level of fame to it. Most people have probably seen one, even if just on TV.

This job seemed like a dream. The manager talked about how the sales team were all great, happy, outgoing people having the time of their lives. They went hiking, played basketball, and made trips to Las Vegas. But none of that had anything to do with the job itself. He talked about people making tons of money in their first week with no experience. Before you get any ideas, this sales job was perfectly conventional. There were no illicit or shady aspects about the merchandise itself.

The manager spent a small portion of his time discussing what the job involved and spent most of the time talking about how wonderful his life was and the lives of all the people at the company.

They were living the dream, supposedly.

After the end of their presentation, the candidates and I felt like they were doing us a favor just by allowing us the privilege of having the chance to work with them.

For a moment while they had me there, I figured—*Why not?* Then I realized, as part of the trial period, they wanted me to work for free. They sold this job so hard to the candidates that they expected us to find new clients and sell products to them. We would only get paid if we made a sale. But in the meantime, we would be going around town, advertising their company and products for them.

Honestly, I didn't truly need the money—if I did, I probably would have jumped on this opportunity to see where it would take me. After all, this was a well-known item. Its reputation for being of high quality and the potential to make some money all made the prospect tempting.

Yet, something bothered me about my whole experience with this company. There was a lack of truthfulness from the very beginning. The advertisement for the position was purposely vague—it didn't even mention sales. It felt strange that the interview lasted two minutes with trivial questions, and then they selected me to move forward. The presentation about the job mainly focused on their incredible lives, feeling more like an infomercial promoting their business rather than discussing the job.

There was falseness in the air.

I was left wondering if the interviews were even real or just staged to appear to look like formal interviews. I was even skeptical about whether all the other candidates for the position were real or if some of them were actors meant to fill up space and help build enthusiasm. This would create the illusion that if all the actors (or seemingly, the other candidates) were excited about the position, I would have to be crazy to let this opportunity pass me by.

This experience served as an important lesson for me. When we don't know who we are, money is a powerful motivator. When you lack your personal will or self-understanding, it becomes an obvious choice to go wherever you will get paid more. If I had not been going to Purdue University and not had a strong sense of being introverted, a thinker, and someone who valued truth, and if I had desperately needed the money, I probably would have gone ahead with this job.

And there is nothing wrong with that job. The point of this story isn't to criticize any job or profession. My point is that when you know yourself, no one else will guide you in a particular direction so easily. But when you don't know yourself, anyone can guide you into doing practically anything.

If I had known myself any less than I did, I might be selling their merchandise right now rather than writing this book.

When you don't know yourself, it's easy for others to tell you who you are. They wanted to convince me that I was the right person for this job. They had turned the tables. Usually, when you go to a job interview, they are looking to filter you out and get rid of you to hire the right person. Instead, in this case, they wanted to include everyone that they could. I can only guess that they struggle to keep their workers, so they want to avoid filtering anyone out before giving them a chance to sell.

I can see now that these companies were in the business of creating their truth. They convince their workers that their company is the best, has the most fun, and makes the most money. Everyone who works there believes that their products are the best and exactly what every customer should have. Upholding this version of truth helps them sell more of the product, attract more motivated salespeople, and make more money.

But this version of truth is not what I am after.

I am not after a convenient truth that helps me to make money. Or a convenient truth that allows me to feel good. Or one that will enable me to live in a lie, feel comfortable, and keep the peace artificially. I would rather pursue what is fully true, not some fabricated lies.

How can we get away from the convenient truths and get closer to our truth? A key step is that we need to stop caring so much about what others think.

Many of us are too concerned with what the people around us think. This is something I see everywhere I go. I think we all care to some extent. But when we care and worry too much about what others will think, we cannot live out our truth. In such cases, we will tend to live out a phony version of ourselves, just trying to be liked by everyone else. Instead, we have to learn to care less what the people around us think. Of course, it's fine to consider others' opinions, especially if they are close friends and family. Still, we should not let their thoughts control our lives either.

This is a cliché, but when you discover your true self, the people around you should like you for who you are. You shouldn't have to live your life as a lie, pretending to be someone you are not, to be liked. You do not have to enjoy all of the same things that your family and friends do. You do not always have to agree with them. It is okay to be your unique and authentic self. And if someone cannot accept this, you may be better off not having them in your life.

Keep in mind that it is possible to be sensitive and aware of others' needs and still be yourself. This can be a challenge. A way to accomplish this is to be firm about what you want and do not want, or what you think and do not think is correct, but you do not need to impose this on others. Just the same, you can accept and listen to what others have to say, but you do not need to allow them to impose their way on you. They can have their way, and you can have yours.

Contrary to what many of us may think, a person who appears weak or even undecided may be stronger than it would seem. When I was much younger, I worried more about what people thought about me, so I often agreed with what people told me in public. However, I was usually quite thoughtful. I realized that they had failed to consider something import-ant, or I would disagree with their point of view privately. I appeared weak-willed in public and easily swayed, but I was very stubborn when it came to my private thoughts. Someone could not sway my opinion so easily.

I still do this sometimes if it is not someone I know, and I do not want to argue. But when I know someone well, I make it a point to speak my mind and let them know what I think. I always mention that these are just my opinions. Or I say that I heard a particular fact somewhere. Often, rather than coming from the position of knowing, I tend to come from the approach of questioning or wondering. I am well aware that none of us has all the facts. I already know what I think about a topic, so I may as well learn what someone else thinks about it and how they came to their conclusions. Just because you stop and hear someone else's perspective does not mean you need to agree.

A common approach I use is rather than vehemently opposing what people say and entering a debate—I prefer to say that I will have to read up on that later. Suppose someone is going in a direction that you are not happy with and which you feel is false. In that case, you may tell them that you are not sure about those sources or that you have also heard conflicting information. Sometimes, it isn't worth getting into a heated debate, and you may also just change the topic after a certain point.

I tend to be happy to go along with what the people around me like to do or want to do. I do not feel the need to force things to go in a particular direction. However, when I know something conflicts with who I am, I have no problem drawing a line and saying that I am not interested.

As an example, let's say I am meeting a couple of friends. During that meeting, an acquaintance of them joins us, and he suggests that they leave to vandalize someone's home that he has a personal problem with. My friends agree to go because they all have issues with this person and want to teach him a lesson.

This is not something I would have to think about. I would simply say that I have to leave and excuse myself. It's not in my nature to cause new problems or act in anger toward someone, and of course, I am not someone who breaks the law. These are all counter to who I am as a person, and so I don't do it. This is not a gray area for me. In the end, they may ask me just to give them a ride—my answer would still be "No." I do not want to be involved.

To continue with this example, I have heard that young people will sometimes vandalize a place, perhaps out of boredom or amusement. Some of them learn after doing such things that it is not a part of their identity. And unfortunately, some may realize that they have no problem breaking the law and move on to committing bigger crimes.

Of course, I do not advocate for committing any crimes, but we all have to find our way to be. Some people will learn to be better only after they have made their mistakes. We have to find our truth, and this is not always a single direct path. When we know our truth, we can simply live this out, and it flows from us. We do not need to worry about figuring out a new situation—we will tend to know the right approach for us to take. There is no single right way to live, of course. But the important thing is to find your own "right way."

Listen to your truth, and it will speak louder and more clearly to you. When we deny our truth and move further away from it, we give it less of a voice, and we end up doing things that are not who we are. Eventually, it is possible to lose who we are if we stray further and further from our truth.

If we are not careful, it is possible to reach a point where we are a stranger to ourselves.

Finding your truth is no easy task. We can all be put in difficult situations sometimes, and we may not know the right course of action to take. But this is why it is vital to *live our truth* through our *everyday actions*. When you handle small life choices as true to yourself as you can, you will more smoothly manage the big life choices.

Understand that conflict can be used as a tool to help you find your truth. Some people do not want any conflict. I tend to avoid it, but conflict is not always destructive. If all you do is avoid conflict, people can push you around, tell you what to do, and disregard you. At some point, you have to be willing to speak up for what is important to you. If your important truths are being cast aside, then it is up to you to make this known. Then, the people around you will be able to understand your perspective better.

Of course, conflict often leads us into emotional reactions, which are part of our truth as well. If you get angry, sad, or anxious at some point, this is an actual experience you are going through. It is up to you to listen to these emotions so that they can help guide you toward where you need to be. The negative emotions are often just pointing out to us that something is not going well. If you are crying regularly, then you have to ask: *What is wrong? What is disturbing me? And how can I better live my truth to overcome this?*

It takes time to get to know yourself. When you are young, have some patience. You need time to remember, uncover, recover, discover, and create yourself. This doesn't happen overnight. When you are uncertain and make a mistake and move away from your truth, this is an opportunity to shift your perspective. When you stray from your truth, if you realize that this has happened, then you can redirect yourself back toward it. Even in moving away from yourself, you can move back toward your true self. There are no mistakes, as long as you use them to guide you back to your true self.

Even as we get older, we should be willing to continue to go deeper into who we are and discover and create new versions of ourselves. As we age, we tend to get set in our ways, but there are no limits to how much we can grow, change, and evolve. In many ways, older people may not be so different from the young. When we get older, we still do not know everything about ourselves, and we should be willing to explore ourselves more deeply.

I would advise this: The old should befriend the young. Men should strive to know women. The outgoing should aim to connect with the introverted. And for all of these, the relationships go both ways. Find someone who will help to illuminate parts of yourself that you didn't even know were there.

In getting to know others, you will better understand yourself. And in getting to know yourself, you will know the right way to live.

KEY QUESTIONS

When You Know Yourself, You Know the Right Way to Be

1. Were you ever led astray because you didn't know yourself well enough? Was this a challenging and valuable life lesson learned?

2. What have been the biggest tests of character, willpower, stamina, intellect, or leadership in your life? What did you learn about yourself?

3. What is something you have learned about yourself that surprised you? If nothing, this is a sign that you could benefit from taking a few more risks.

4. When was the last time someone tried to convince you that they knew you better than you knew yourself? Were they right or not?

5. Are you being guided by your inner truth and life force, or has some external motivator such as money, status, power, or another desire been leading you up to now?

TAKE ACTION TODAY

When You Know Yourself, You Know the Right Way to Be

Action: **Ask yourself what your core reason for existence is.** This may involve your personal growth, helping someone, or meeting your professional duties. It could also involve a calling, such as a religious goal, teaching, or parenting. Otherwise, it may involve an overarching value that is more important to you than anything else, such as Truth, Love, Family, or Wisdom.

Try to forget for a moment what anyone else has directed you toward being. What is it that YOU are here to do? This may be something that will emanate from your inner core. It will shine like a light from within and not be something you must attempt or work toward.

Today, write out your life purpose in two or three sentences. You can draft something longer if you wish, but try to keep it concise in the end. This will help you to stay focused. What is it you are here to do in this life that you have been given?

Reason: If you do not know your WHY, then it is difficult to know yourself. We can all take action and work toward making progress in some area of our lives, but what is the deeper reason that what you do or focus on truly matters?

Tip: When you have your core reason for existence, write it down and reflect on it periodically. As you grow or evolve, it is okay to revisit your statement, revise it, or even rewrite it. If you find it very difficult to come up with your reason for existence, keep in mind that your life's goal may be to figure this out for now. You may need to explore more of yourself and more of the world before you can know your WHY.

When You Know the Right Way to Be, You Will Live Your Truth Every Day

"Let's tell the truth to people. When people ask, 'How are you?' have the nerve sometimes to answer truthfully. You must know, however, that people will start avoiding you because, they, too, have knees that pain them and heads that hurt and they don't want to know about yours. But think of it this way: If people avoid you, you will have more time to meditate and do fine research on a cure for whatever truly afflicts you."

— Maya Angelou, *Letter to My Daughter*

As the prior section discussed, when you know yourself, you know the right way to be. This means that in understanding yourself, you will know the right actions that you need to take in your life. Your choices will not feel like there are infinite options, and you must simply select some arbitrary course of action. Instead, the truth will flow from inside of you.

Understand that ultimately when you know how to be, you will live your truth every day. This is a profound idea. By knowing yourself and knowing how to be, you will be led to your truth every single day.

You will get to a point where instead of thinking so much about your life and what you are going through (if this is something you tend to do), you will simply be. This means that if someone says something to annoy you, you will be able to exist in that moment of annoyance. There will be no need to wonder how to get back at him or appear as if you are not bothered or say something witty that diffuses the tension. There will be no need to think about this.

For example, what if someone said: "Wow, looks like someone bought his/her shoes at the Dollar store" while talking about you.

If you know who you are, this shouldn't bother you. I think it is natural in such a case to take this in a light-hearted way.

You may quip: "Yeah, that's where I do most of my shopping, how did you know?" or "I'm saving up for a Ferrari—we all have to make sacrifices to make that dream come true."

You don't have to be cunning to be yourself. You could say: "I'm busy with work right now, but feel free to tell me all about it later during the break," acting as if what he said was of no importance because actually, that is the case.

When you know your truth and what you stand for in this life, these responses will come to you easily. However, the less we know ourselves, the harder it is to find a response. If you don't know who you are, you may take his comments very personally. Perhaps what is happening is that you don't know yourself, so you feel the weight of his remarks heavily. You think that you have been defined as someone who has a lousy style or who is too poor to afford better shoes, and it hurts. Unfortunately, you may not have your definition of who you are, so his definition sticks with you, and you get angry.

Then you want to get back at him and hurt him. But a part of his personal truth has become that tearing people down with snarky comments is fun, so he probably has books at home full of witty one-liners. In the end, trying to beat him at his own game won't work. You will feel worse and worse about yourself. The annoying person has won when you don't know yourself. He has just highlighted that you don't know yourself, and he has defined you because you never decided who you were for yourself.

In knowing how to be, you will not have to worry about annoying people like this. New and unexpected situations will not be troublesome anymore. You will know yourself well enough to know how to handle most new situations with ease. You will be able to find your one true authentic voice.

You will be unflappably you.

If your truth is loving, you will respond lovingly: "Wow—you must be having a bad day if you're worried about my shoes. Have a great day anyway, friend."

If your truth is confidence, you will respond confidently: "I only use my nice shoes for special occasions, like for date nights," said with a smile and getting back to work.

If your truth is happiness, you will respond happily: "I guess these shoes are a bit old, but I'm happy with what I have."

When I began my writing career many years ago, I wondered what "voice" I would write in, as if I had to pick how I wanted to sound. Now, I do not worry about this. My voice is just the words that naturally flow out of me, as a part of my truthful self. The words are finding me as much as I am finding them. I am not concerned with making my words sound more serious, entertaining, or expert-like. The words are what they are—what matters to me is whether I am conveying my truth to you. Hopefully, my truth will connect with something more universal that we can all relate to.

You are getting my one, true, authentic voice. I am genuine in all my words, whether spoken or written.

When you know yourself, your truth shines through not just in your words but also in your thoughts, actions, habits, and every aspect of your being.

None of us know ourselves completely, of course. Recall that we have a subconscious part of ourselves that we do not have access to. You may uncover some of this hidden side of yourself by reading this book, but it's uncertain if we can reveal all of it.

The parts of me that I do not fully know and understand, I am okay with. I am fine with learning and exploring and figuring things out as I go, as we all have to on this human journey. The only way to know everything about yourself would be to have had every possible experience, which of course, is not possible. The next best thing you can do is to have more varied types of experiences. For example, you may try out different hobbies, books, sports, games, conversational styles, words, and visit new places. Something else that can help is to make different types of friends. If your friends are usually of the same socioeconomic status and in the same profession, you may try to meet people who come from different walks of life instead.

When you know yourself, you will gain confidence. But don't be over-confident—there is always more to discover about yourself. In knowing yourself, you will find that not everyone has this luxury. You will meet someone new and know right away if this person does not know himself. There is not a straightforward way for me to explain this. It has to do with body language, eye contact, and even tone of voice. Most of us get a sense of this, but we cannot always put it into words.

Nonetheless, in knowing yourself and capturing your truth, you will be in a better position to help others move toward their truth. When you figure out Your Personal Truth, you free up brain space to pay more attention to the people around you, and you see what they are going through.

You may see that a coworker always seems available to take on more work and never says "No." But if you open up your perception, you may find that she is well beyond her limit and is on the verge of breaking down. This coworker's version of the truth is that if she says "No," she could be fired or found to be incompetent. She is insecure. And the reality is that for most of us, we all have some level of insecurity. No one is perfect, and so it is natural to feel insecure about an area of our lives in which we do not feel as accomplished as we would like.

Perhaps you have your life figured out, and you have set hard limits and boundaries, and you often do say "No." You work hard, but you do not want your life to be ruled by work. Because you say "no" to some requests, most of that work ends up going to your coworker, who is overloaded. In that case, in understanding this truth, you would have to evaluate whether you should take on more work to make things fair. Of course, there are other options—you may talk to your supervisor to help reach an agreement that can work for everyone. Or you may help your coworker to organize herself better.

After finding your truth, you will need to understand that everything you do still affects the world around you. Consider that in living out your truth, you may be helping others to live out theirs as well, or in some cases, you may be an obstacle to someone else's truth. So you will have to ask if your truth can coexist with other people's. In some cases, it may, and in others, you may be in too much of an opposition, and there may only be room for one truth to shine through.

Take some time to make sure that your personal truths represent the actual truth. Just because a perspective makes you feel good or provides some short-term benefit, or everyone around you agrees with it, does not make it accurate. The truth runs much deeper. Ask yourself if you are just following a convenient path or the actual truth. I have repeated this message throughout the book because I believe it is quite easy to forget. And we must avoid falling into old patterns that drag us away from our truth.

Sometimes living out our truth is not easy. It's easy when things are running smoothly. If society is a stream of perspectives, and your viewpoint mostly flows along with that of society, then you can live out your truth comfortably and without too much difficulty. But if society is flowing one way, and your truth conflicts with that, then living out your truth can be a challenge as you swim against society's current.

If people disagree with you, you have to ask whether what you believe is important enough to spend your time and energy trying to convince others. Do you need to convince them? Is that important? Or is it fine for you to have your truth that does not necessarily line up with what most people have in mind?

I do have my personal truths, and I'm not sure others would always agree with me. I have thought deeply about this life and reality, and I am trying to understand the whole truth. I don't believe that I have it, but I am not interested in following one specific way of thought. I am just interested in figuring out the way that works for me. I don't need anyone to follow what I think or believe. Also, I don't need anyone to lead me. However, I look to leaders for inspiration and direction while figuring things out in my way.

I don't think my way is the right way for most people. It may work for some and not for others. By spending so much time in my mind and thoughts, I run the risk of considering some ideas that others have already proven to be wrong. But part of my system involves questioning and reconsidering to define and refine what the truth is.

What I have found is that Truth is a process and a journey, not a destination.

In the end, reality is complex. There is truth and falseness wrapped up in everything. Imagine if I were to tell you a story, any story. Then that story is true because it is the way I experienced it. Still, it is false because it fails to factor in the perspectives of all the other people who may have been involved in the story. Have you ever heard a story from one perspective and found yourself agreeing with that person's viewpoint? Then you heard someone else's side of the story, and it made you reconsider everything you had initially heard? This is what I am referring to. Ultimately, I believe there is some truth and some falseness in everything.

Our goal in pursuing our truth is to figure out how much of what happens in your life is true or false. If you are learning something, how much is true, and how much is false? What about if someone tells you a story?

And here is a challenging one. When it comes to your treasured thoughts, which ones are valid, and which ones are not?

When you figure this out, you will come to live your truth every day through your actions.

You will be the living expression of your truth.

KEY QUESTIONS

When You Know the Right Way to Be,
You Will Live Your Truth Every Day

1. What is a deep truth that guides your life? Is it love, happiness, knowledge, discipline, a particular skill, or talent? What is it that is expressed in every breath you take?

2. Have you tried a wide enough range of activities to know yourself? Have you experienced various hobbies, sports, books, movies, locations, friendships, and so on? Did you need that wide range of experiences to find your truth, or were you able to make up your mind more easily?

3. What is something important to you, but you are not sure if it is fully valid? Perhaps you wish it were true, and you try to make it true in your life, but deep down, you think there may be some falseness in the idea.

4. Do you feel like you have to work hard to figure out what to say, what tone to say it in, and to try to manage how other people see you? Or are you able to let the truth flow out of you without needing to think about it that deeply?

5. What is a truth that is worth arguing over, or perhaps even fighting for? And what is one that is not worth it?

TAKE ACTION TODAY

When You Know the Right Way to Be,
You Will Live Your Truth Every Day

Action: **Today, aim to live your authentic self through all of your actions.** If your truth is kindness, then commit to being kind in everything you do. If your truth is doing your best, then commit to that. If your truth is empathy and human understanding, then go the extra mile to make sure that you deeply understand the people around you. For any personal truth that you hold in your life, commit to it today, in a way that you perhaps never have.

As this can feel like a Herculean task, pick one Truth, and start there.

Reason: Often, we have an idea in our minds that we are kind, truthful, or hardworking. But when an obstacle presents itself, we may give up easily and back down, casting our truth or our principles aside. Instead, we have to rise to the challenges of our lives and commit to living our truth through every action we take. This is how we get to higher levels of truth in our lives. Many of us tend to lie to ourselves, thinking that we are the type of person who lives by a particular value or principle. Still, when faced with everyday life challenges, we may forget them and take the easy road. Instead, **I challenge you to live your truth with every breath, action, and step you take.**

Tip: Practice being more conscious in your actions and more objective in how you see yourself. It's easy to make excuses and take it easy on yourself, but try to see things from someone else's perspective. Maybe you were kind, but could you have done more? Perhaps you tried to stand up for someone, but should you have been more firm? Or maybe you worked hard on some goal, but in the end, you gave up when you got tired of working on it. Many people *say* the right things. They all say things that sound reasonable and helpful, but when we scrutinize a person's day-to-day actions, often they are not following their own words. It's much more challenging to *live* by your thoughts and words than to produce ones that *sound* good.

147

Find Your Personal Truth in the Universe of All Possible Truths

"If someone is able to show me that what I think or do is not right, I will happily change, for I seek the truth, by which no one was ever truly harmed. It is the person who continues in his self-deception and ignorance who is harmed."

— Marcus Aurelius, *Meditations*

I view the universe as a living, organic being. It is guiding us toward our truth every day. Somehow, human beings are simply stubborn, and we are capable of moving along the false paths over and over, despite the universe gently guiding us toward truth.

To me, the Universe and Truth are the same things. We process the world and universe in so many different ways—we have senses that help us gain information, emotions, intuition, and logic. We may defer to leaders and respected organizations, or in some cases we may observe nature to learn from that. There are so many ways to process the world, but none of them gives us the whole truth.

Many people who get full of anger and rage do this because they have just found one truth, their perspective, and have somehow forgotten that there are other ways to be.

Think of the word "infanticide." This means to kill an infant. The thought may make you upset, and you may think that the idea should not even exist. It is horrific, right?

Consider that in Stone Age societies, this was viewed as a responsibility to help manage populations and make sure that every person in a tribe could be properly cared for. Resources were limited, and they viewed infanticide as necessary for the greater good. In modern society, there is no need for it. So we think this is misguided, and essentially it is considered murder. But keep in mind that just because it is difficult for us to understand their perspective does not make us right and them wrong.

The point here is that there are many different ways to perceive the same fact—and this is how some of us can develop truths that conflict with each other.

Ultimately, the values that we have are assigned by *us* as a function of the human perspective. Everything important to us is defined this way simply because humans live in human societies with human needs and desires. This is just assumed.

If someone on the streets asks me what my job is, I would never respond:

"A job? Why do you humans find it necessary to perform arbitrary tasks to earn paper with dead presidents that enable you to acquire objects that serve little purpose?"

Somehow, that type of response seems to come from an alien, from someone who does not connect with the reality that every human lives. Most of us hope not to perform "arbitrary tasks" but instead look to find a way to help other humans with something they need or want. The "paper with dead presidents" is money that is quite useful to have. And of course, many of us would like to acquire not just "objects that serve little purpose," but hopefully things that will help clothe, shelter, and entertain us.

Yet from the alien's perspective, he is correct in finding all of our habits silly. For an imaginary alien being, nothing that humans do makes any sense. An alien lifeform will hold different truths than us humans.

It is easy to forget that we are all working from a human perspective because we mostly interact with humans. We can only talk to other humans. Other conscious animals cannot discuss their views with us. So we tend to forget about them, or at least to disregard them.

To humans, the human perspective is what matters. We choose what we value, and we decide what our truths are.

Choosing our truths can be challenging because the potential realities that exist are practically infinite. And it is up to us to evaluate them, distinguish which are more objective and accurate, and worthy of our time and attention. As the title of this chapter states, I would like you to find your truth in the universe of all possible truths.

I believe that the universe is true by default. Everything that the universe encompasses is a form of truth. From the universe's perspective, falseness would be anything that does not exist within the known universe. This may be strange to think about but stay with me.

You may think, of course, there is falseness within the universe. But think of this another way. If my friend Robert tells me "7 + 2 = 11", I will say that is wrong, and he should recalculate this. Yet, in another theoretical sense, "7 + 2 = 11" is true because the thought has been created in the universe. It is true in the sense that the idea exists in Robert's mind. One person, somewhere, has formed the thought, making it his unique truth.

Let's say that Robert's parents taught him that 7 + 2 = 11 when he was a child. Every day, Robert was quizzed on his math, and it was in sync with the math that you and I know. But for some reason, Robert's parents emphasized that 7 + 2 = 11. When Robert believed in this equation, they congratulated him for getting this difficult question correct.

Later on, as Robert went to school, his teachers tried to teach him that actually, 7 + 2 = 9. But somehow, Robert was stubborn, and he became convinced that he was right to believe 7 + 2 = 11, even though his teachers and other students seemed sure that this was wrong.

Finally, as Robert grew older and got into high school, he realized the silliness of his ways. To do math, he needed to agree with the people around him on certain ideas. And one day, he realized that in his mind, 7 + 2 = 11 was still correct, but for the sake of communicating effectively with others, he would think of "11" as a 9 in that particular case. Having learned 7 + 2 = 11 from a young age, Robert visualized the "11" as what most of us call a 9. He imagined it correctly but just called the number by a different name.

In a way, Robert was right all along; 7 + 2 = 11 was right, for him, in his world, in his mind, by his definitions of numbers (which could change depending on the calculation).

To me, truth is a form of existence. Anything that happens, or is thought, is true, at least from a particular person's perspective.

It is up to us to pursue our inner truth in a personal, spiritual way, searching for the ones that matter most to us. The universe is showing us all possible truths every day. I can find someone who believes anything if I look hard enough. So all these possible ways of being exist in the universe. It doesn't make them all True, in the absolute, universal sense.

But since no one can attain the absolute, universal truth about anything, what truly matters in this limited lifetime is Your Personal Truth.

How do you know what is true for you? It will make sense to you with all of your sensory and intellectual abilities. It will match up with all your prior experiences. You will be pulled toward your truth as if there were a magnet pointing you in that direction.

Somewhere in another part of the universe, to an alien being, everything about you is false. On his planet, they don't breathe oxygen. They don't communicate through words, and they don't share our ethical beliefs. To his people, we don't exist because they have never seen us. And to us, they don't exist because we have never seen them. We are false to each other because we have never experienced one another.

Truth is what is there.

Falseness is what is not.

What do you want to attract more of? What do you value or want to value more? What matters? Who matters? What makes you feel alive? What type of people, places, or things do you naturally connect with? All of this is the universe pointing you toward your truth.

Find your truth, your Tao, your path, and pursue it.

Yet, never forget that your truth does not align with everyone's perspective. If you have never been lonely, then this does not mean that loneliness does not exist in the universe. It just means that it does not exist for you in your universe. It means that you will struggle to relate to the truth of loneliness.

What do you relate or not relate to?

How about people who are rich or poor, funny or serious, disabled or enabled, emotional or stable, rational or irrational, rude or polite, intellectual or lacking formal education, hardworking or lazy, nature-loving or homebodies, friendly or antagonizing, and so on.

In the end, I think we are like mirrors, looking for ourselves in the universe. When I was a child, I felt like the embodiment of myself in the universe was a racecar driver. All I ever wanted to do was drive and race. Living on the edge seemed like it would be a lot of fun. As I couldn't drive, this meant I was attracted to playing video games that involved driving and racing.

By the time I was old enough to drive, I was satisfied to drive a typical car and didn't feel the need to race. I knew that racing in a game versus in real life would not be the same thing.

Now, I like to think, learn, and improve myself and help others do the same. This truth is expressed through my writing and in everything I do in my life. I believe I have been searching the universe for people like myself. I have found or attracted some friends who have similar thought processes to mine. I want to be challenged to think in new directions. So I often meet and attract friends who feel similarly and who are willing to disagree amicably at times, as long as it helps us all grow intellectually or spiritually.

Of course, we must remember that just because we surround ourselves with people who think in a certain way does not mean we are right and everyone else is wrong. All it means is that we have found our truth.

As we have been speaking of the universe, I think it helps to consider when you have found a universal truth. Universal truths are typically the actual Truth.

Isaac Newton's laws of motion were so powerful because they expressed truths about the universe itself. For our practical life purposes, a universal truth does not always have to apply in 100% of cases. Very few facts will apply to that level.

We cannot access universal truths most of the time. What we can access are personal truths. These are the truths that work for us. What we believe are Universal truths are often an illusion and end up being filled with exceptions when you look closely enough.

This is an example of a truth that can seem universal: *You should never lie.*

In reality, it is not universal because many people believe lying is acceptable in some instances. Perhaps you lie to prevent someone's feelings from being hurt, for example.

In your life, can you think of any personal truths? I will write some here just as examples to give you an idea of what may work for you. Perhaps some of these are true for you, and some not:

- I should walk away if someone insults me because, in the past, I regretted getting into petty arguments
- I should focus on who I love and put my energy there, rather than on the people who I do not like
- My family will always be there for me, no matter what
- There is always a way to make progress—all hope is never lost
- People who can only see the negative side of things just need more positivity in their life to help shift their perspective
- I should always know why I am doing something—that way, if I make a mistake, I can justify how my actions seemed reasonable at the time
- What matters to me is being able to create art—no matter what happens, I always want to make time in my life for this

What are your truths? Think of all the experiences you have ever had. Which ones stand out to you? What are some of the highlights of your life? What are some of the great lessons you have learned through your experiences? What truths shine through as a result of these experiences?

Consider different topics. What are your truths regarding family, friends, work, ethics, values, emotions, love, health, success, responsibility, happiness, peace, and understanding?

Just because I have used the word "truth" so much in this book—as, of course, that is the topic at hand—does not mean that I take the meaning lightly. A Personal Truth is the most critical truth because this is the truth for you in your life. You can use it as a guiding light to lead you because you know it to be the case with every fiber of your being. As I already stated, you know it to be true logically, intuitively, based on experience, based on what friends and family believe, and readings.

When the universe is pointing you toward a particular truth, you should listen to it.

These truths do not need to be the most profound statements ever—they are important just in the fact that they are your truths.

Truth can be powerful because when you believe something, you tend to create that as your reality. Understand that there is great responsibility in your beliefs and truths. They shape the reality around us.

Because our truths are such a great responsibility, I aim to keep things positive with everything that I focus on in life. We stray along the wrong paths when we allow our truths to be filled with negativity—hate, dread, meaninglessness, pain, and so on. Negativity is a reality of life, but we should not allow such truths to rule us.

Not to get too grim here, but perhaps you have lost a loved one at some point in your life. This could have been someone very close to you. If this has not happened, then consider how such an experience could impact you.

This thought may come across a person's mind going through this type of situation: "I can't believe this happened to me. I'm not sure I can keep on living like I used to. I'm not sure life is even worth it anymore."

Allowing these thoughts to echo in your mind every day would make them your truth, your reality. This would be your "7 + 2 = 11" For you, these negative thoughts could become your reality. They could imprint and stay stuck in your mind if you became convinced that they were true.

The longer those thoughts get stuck in your mind, the longer you may dread getting up in the morning, living your everyday life, continuing with your goals, and helping loved ones.

And, of course, it may be natural to get sucked into that during a grieving period. But eventually, we must reevaluate this perspective and replace it with a more positive and helpful truth.

Perhaps you could think: "I lost someone dear to me, and I must never forget the times we cherished. I have to remember the positive spirit of the person who left us and try to pass that on through my life and actions. This person who is no longer physically here can live on through me, every day."

Our truths provide meaning. This meaning energizes us to action and helps keep us in positive spirits. But if you find ones that do not give you meaning, that are not actionable, not positive, and not productive, those truths will not help you. Such perspectives are filled with falseness, and you have to get rid of them, extricate them from your mind, your life, and your spirit.

When you have a thought, it is true in the sense that it has happened in the universe. It exists and therefore has some truth in it. However, when I have a thought that is not useful or positive, or productive in any way, I remind myself that this thought is not necessarily true. I do not need to give it the power of truth.

Thoughts are just an elementary form of truth. We get to decide whether to transform our thoughts into action. If a thought is not helping you, prepare to abandon it and replace it with the truths that will help you.

As you have learned, we can select some of our truths. These are personal truths. But do not take this to mean that you can make up whatever you want to believe. We should also consider reality and what is happening around us.

Consider all of this, but do not forget your imagination. Think about what is there in the universe, what exists, and what your senses are telling you. Keep that in mind. But you can also attempt to imagine an even better truth for yourself.

Maybe everyone in your life is stuck and headed for disaster. And perhaps they try to convince you that the same is true for you, that you will be a loser no matter what you do. Those thoughts and words of theirs are like a curse they are trying to place on you. If they can convince you, it will become your truth, and you will be destined for disaster. Misery loves company, so perhaps they just want you to join them.

To rise up and become greater than the people around you, you would have to understand that the personal truth of the people around you, the idea that you are destined for failure, is false.

But seeing it as false is not enough. It's challenging to take a thought in your mind and label it as false. This is equivalent to asking you to avoid thinking of *pink elephants*. It's hard to do.

Instead, it's better to overwrite those false statements in your life. Overwrite them with your truths.

And it's okay if your truths are wrong or if they are not 100% accurate. We are all human.

Remember that there is truth and falseness in every statement. My mind was somehow built to see the truth. Because of that, I see falseness too. As soon as someone makes a statement, I immediately see the falseness in it.

For example, any time I hear a statement that begins with "everyone" or "never," I immediately know that these statements are only partly factual. Often, these words are used to exaggerate, as they cannot be taken literally.

As a typical example, someone might say, "You never keep your promises," probably in anger. Still, most of us keep our promises at least some of the time, making the statement unlikely to be true.

As another example of seeing the falseness in simple statements, my friend Amy sometimes says, "I love olives."

The falseness here is that Amy only likes green olives. Also, she only wants the fancy expensive ones and when they are well seasoned. And, of course, they should come with the pits removed. And she only likes to eat a serving or two of them, not to ruin her appetite.

So you tell me, does Amy really "love olives?"

Saying something that is 100% true can be a real challenge. This is because there are limitations to virtually any statement that anyone could make.

If you are wondering, I keep most of these thoughts to myself as they come up through the day. I do what I can to keep my friends, so I wouldn't bother Amy with all of my speculations on whether she genuinely "loves olives" or not.

To see the limitations of every statement or potential truth just slows down the day. It makes us lose confidence—as you may think: *What do I know if I can't even say "I love olives" without doubting myself.*

That is far from the message I want you to come away with.

Doubt is powerful and useful, but there is no reason to doubt with many aspects of life. If you love something or someone, you probably know this with conviction, and it doesn't help you to question too much. If you have a grand goal that you've spent years trying to achieve and have almost accomplished it, there is not much of a need to doubt your motivations. Just finish what you started.

When you are uncertain about something, and it could make a significant impact on your life, perhaps you should doubt and make an effort to figure out your truth. But to find that truth, you have to see the falseness for all it is, trying to lead you astray.

Just consider that maybe some of that "falseness" is part of a universe of truths, and you have to find Your Personal Truth.

KEY QUESTIONS

Find Your Personal Truth in the Universe of All Possible Truths

1. Is there something true for you, but it does not seem to be true for most other people?
2. Have you ever felt strongly that you were being guided in a particular direction by your inner truth, but you went against it? How did you feel, and what happened?
3. Are any truths in your life working against you? Perhaps they are too negative, not practical, or attracting too many problems. What can you do about this?
4. If your personal truth is ultimately just your perspective, are you willing to acknowledge and accept that other people in the world will have conflicting truths of their own?
5. Are there some truths that are so powerful for you that you are convinced that they must be universally true for all humans or all of the universe?

TAKE ACTION TODAY

Find Your Personal Truth in the Universe of All Possible Truths

Action: **Today, look for an object that represents what your truth used to be. Then look for one that represents your current truth. And also, look for one that represents your future truth.** These may be objects that you currently own or that you have recently seen somewhere.

You do not need to have these objects in your possession, but you just need to keep them in mind. Where did your truth used to be? Where is it now? Where is it headed in the future? Considering different objects can help you to perceive any changes more clearly.

Another way to think of this is to focus on your values, priorities, or important people. Then, consider what these were five years ago, what they are today, and what you think they will be in five more years. Can you visualize such transformations in your life more clearly when you focus on something tangible?

Reason: The universe is vast in all the truths that it holds, so it can help to think of your life's Truth as a path. When you see yourself not as a static being but as a dynamic one that can grow and evolve, you will be in a better position to capture your truth.

Tip: If you need more ideas for objects, you may look online through sites that contain many images or objects. Consider Google Images, for example. Otherwise, you may simply be observant and pay attention to all of the things around you on a typical day. Perhaps one of them will inspire you. Don't limit yourself to thinking small. The Statue of Liberty is an object. And for our purposes, so is the sea, and so is the sun.

Explore the Falseness Within You and Beyond You to Get Rid of It

> "It is always the false that makes you suffer, the false desires and fears, the false values and ideas, the false relationships between people. Abandon the false and you are free of pain; truth makes happy, truth liberates."
>
> — Sri Nisargadatta Maharaj

First, what is falseness? You have made it this far in a book about finding Your Personal Truth. But now, we have to ask, what is non-truth? What is falseness?

The falseness is simply anything that moves you away from yourself. It is anything that is making you less of yourself. If it does not sync up with your emotions, feelings, intuition, logic, upbringing, and personal perspective, it can potentially introduce falseness into your life.

We cannot immediately decide that just because something is new and different from what we are used to, it must be false. But we should attempt to understand every single part of ourselves. When we know ourselves fully, then what is true and false for us will be clear.

Truth is the way things are supposed to be, at least for you in your life. Falseness is everything else. When you *Know Yourself Deeply*, you will develop an immediate sense, a flow for what is true for you and what is not.

I am hypersensitive to deception, and so it is natural for me to move toward my truth every day. When I detect any kind of deception in someone, this shows me that here is a path that leads to falseness. Any time I have ignored a sign of deception and decided to move forward with developing a friendship or pursuing a business deal, I ended up regretting it. One act that contradicts truth tends to lead to another and another.

For example, some people may exaggerate their capabilities. Others may try to convince you of something too much, even being willing to lie to you to try to get you to take action or to buy something. Sometimes people will pretend to like you to your face and then spread rumors or talk about you behind your back. When I see blatant deception, I keep in mind that this is a path that will just lead me away from truth.

Suppose I connect with such a deceptive individual. In that case, I will find myself pretending to like this person who is pretending to like me, and I will have entered a pact of falseness. Or suppose I purchase an item where the salesperson is making exaggerated claims. In that case, I will be supporting these people, funding them so that they can lie to more and more people, and take their money undeservedly. Otherwise, if I befriend someone who often lies, I may find myself lying to him and other people, as the habit becomes easy to develop.

Taking one step into falseness just tends to lead to many, many more, until we are sucked into a life of falseness.

I prefer to avoid such paths that will lead me deeper into falseness. Instead, I identify the falseness, and I remove it from my life.

How about you? Have you ever thought about the falseness within you? Or the falseness in your life?

We must learn to explore the falseness within ourselves. Our minds tend to create false perspectives naturally. We are so sure that we understand, but we tend to grasp so little. New knowledge and research always reveal that the things we thought to be true were actually false. Maybe they were just 1% wrong, and a minor correction was needed. In other cases, perhaps they were 99% false, and we needed to throw away our old thinking processes and change our understanding completely.

When I was a teenager, some rebellious peers enjoyed finding a single exception to a rule, then getting in the face of the teacher. Then they would say, "See, what you taught me was nonsense. It doesn't work for me." Often, these teens simply lacked experience and perspective. They assumed that if they tried something once and failed, this proved an idea to be wrong. Perhaps the statement the teacher had made was 90% true, meaning it would apply perfectly well in 90% of cases and not so well the rest of the time. A single exception does not necessarily prove that an idea is wrong, however.

In reality, what matters is our pattern of experience. These experiences make up our fingerprint of being in this world. The things that are closer to 100% true are the ones we are most certain about. For example, perhaps you have some stable personality characteristics.

Let's consider personality more deeply, as clearly this is a significant part of what makes us who we are and what encompasses our truth.

The Big 5 Personality Traits that psychologists have identified are:

Openness—How open to new experiences are you?
Conscientiousness—How organized and hardworking are you?
Extroversion—How much do you prefer to be around others?
Agreeableness—How much do you tend to trust and help others?

Neuroticism—How prone to anxiety and feeling emotionally unstable are you?

These personality traits tend to be stable throughout life. The traits seem to fall on a scale where some people are more or less open and more or less conscientious. Many people will also fall in the middle of the scale. For example, not everyone is entirely extroverted or introverted. They may be slightly introverted, or slightly extroverted, or right in the middle.

As a result of the lives we live, we may go through a wide range of human experiences—times that involve sadness, happiness, love, and trials and tribulations. However, our personalities either do not change much, or they may change gradually.

As an example of how someone may change in personality when I was younger, I was much less open and more introverted. In time, I have shifted to being more open and less introverted. I am sure that I am still on the introverted side, but I am much more willing and interested in socializing with new people than I used to be. Perhaps this is common, as I've met many other people who have experienced a shift toward extroversion throughout their lives.

Even though I am changing, I don't believe that I have been becoming a different person. In reality, I may have just been shifting back into who I was. Sometimes I wonder if we are born with a particular kind of spirit, or at least that we develop this from a young age. And then, along the way, somehow, we forget who we truly are. Then we have to work on finding our true selves once again. That is the challenge of our lives.

I sometimes think: *What would 10-year-old me think about my life now? Or 20-year-old me? Would they think I made good choices to get where I am today? Or would they be disappointed? What would 65-year-old me think?*

Why do I care about what 10-year-old me thinks? I suspect it's because, at 10, I knew few things, but what I knew, I would have been sure that it was true.

At 20, I had learned so much compared to when I was a child, but much of what I knew was perhaps misguided, and I may have strayed from my truth.

I'm not sure if I ever lost myself or was on the path toward losing myself. In reality, every step we take is just a part of the journey toward our truth.

By losing your Tao or your way, you will naturally need to find your way back to your personal truth. So in losing yourself, you find yourself.

I also sometimes think about my 65-year-old self because I imagine that this may be a version of me that has figured out as much as he ever will. The year will be 2050. This version of myself will know more about who I am as a person because I presume that I will have been tested more deeply by that age. I will have experienced loss, pain, and perhaps regret, injury, or illness. I hope the positives outweigh the negatives, of course, but any life will have its share of hardship.

By 65 years old, I will have captured much more of the truth and attained a deeper understanding of life than I have been able to at 35 years old.

A year ago, I decided to enter a meditative state and communicate with the 65-year-old version of myself. Yes, you can read that sentence one more time to let that sink in.

I entered a meditative state. Then I asked for the most valuable wisdom that my 65-year-old self could bestow upon me. He told me: "Do not look to me for answers. You want to believe that there are easy, simple, magical solutions just like everyone else. This is the flaw, where flocks of people want to chase that. In reality, learning is difficult, slow, and learned through hard life lessons. Do not be afraid to live out those hard lessons for yourself. Learn by living."

Take that wisdom however it suits you. I found it insightful, as it was true for me.

Unfortunately, the falseness in our human lives will not go away. Instead, I feel its forces are growing, and truth is taking the backseat in our lives.

There is falseness every day, everywhere we go. Often, I hear people say that you are supposed to be a certain way. To me, this is falseness. We should educate someone on manners, responsibility, and success without saying that you have to act in a certain way or perform a specific set of actions to meet your goals.

Perhaps for children in school, the teachers need to create so many rules to keep order. However, we make and follow so many rules for so many situations in daily life that there may not be much room to breathe and be ourselves. Lately, I have found that I prefer to forget about the rules, at least sometimes. By rules, I am not talking about essential laws of society. Instead, I refer to unwritten rules such as needing to tip a specific amount, responding to a greeting in a certain way, or being polite when others expect you to be.

As an example, I once saw a man in a restaurant chastising his girlfriend for using the wrong fork, then it was for chewing with her mouth open, and then for not using her napkin the right way. At first, I thought he was right, as it is important to have some principles of politeness and order everywhere we go. And then I wondered, why should we feel forced into following societal rules that strip us of our personality and selves and make us all into the same thing? In the end, I thought that he could mention his concerns to her, and that was fine. But in being so openly judgmental, it seemed he was shaming her into following his views on etiquette. That part seemed wrong. It sends the message that "if you don't follow my arbitrary rules for civility, then I can make your life miserable."

I don't see any problem with most rules of etiquette. I think for those who want to follow them completely, that is great. But I do not want to go to a place, whether it's a restaurant, gas station, or friend's house, and be struck with anxiety over needing to follow every rule. Then if I fail to do so, perhaps I would be labeled a classless barbarian. I do what I can, live by my truth, try to be considerate, and leave it at that. And for situations that call for too many rules, perhaps it will be best for me to avoid them.

I mention rules because many times in life, I have found them restricting my truth. "We are supposed to do things this way," they tell me. I have a creative mind that wants to question, and take things in new directions, and challenge the order, and so I sometimes find it difficult to accept the rules as they are.

Being overly rule-focused can lead us to falseness. This is all I want you to be aware of.

Ask yourself: What is restricting my truth and leading me to falseness?

Is it a particular type of person with a strong personality that tends to lead you astray from your values and life goals? Is it a set of rules that you find arbitrary but all of the people around you believe to be important? Is it that you have not decided on a purpose or path for yourself? Is it that you often prefer to lie to keep the peace rather than tell people how you feel? Do you find yourself getting dragged into petty arguments online, perhaps with people you do not know in real life? Are you telling yourself the same story about yourself every day that keeps you in the same spot you do not want to be in? Have you been compromising on your key values?

Here is something difficult to consider, but it's worth keeping in mind.

Is there a grand illusionist in your life, carefully planting ideas into your head just to get you to agree with them? Is there someone or some group trying to make you believe what they want you to? Perhaps it helps them when you buy into their version of the truth. Consider an overbearing romantic partner who convinces you that you are the problem because you are not living up to his or her standards. What about ruthless advertising agencies that bombard you with ideas that make you feel as if you lack something, which they conveniently happen to sell. How about news agencies? Are they providing you with facts or just providing you with a narrative that satisfies their owners? Are they reporting the news or making up their version of "truth?"

Remember the earlier chapter, *No One Can Give You Truth—You Must Seek It For Yourself.*

Who or where is the illusionist in your life, pulling strings, making you doubt the actual truth, and presenting you with their convenient "facts"? Think of this deeply. Billions of dollars are spent every day, selling you a version of the truth. At some point, we have to question and ask ourselves: *What is the actual truth?*

I have already stated that convenient stories are not necessarily the truth. Now, consider that just because there are images placed in front of you, this does not mean they are true. In today's age, pictures and voices can be manipulated by technology. There is less certainty than ever. And so when you see massive groups of people following convenient "truths," remember once again that this does not make them correct.

We have to learn to question more deeply and think more critically to discover our truth in a world directing us toward falseness. Most of my books have been written with such goals in mind. You are welcome to view a list of those titles at the end of this book.

KEY QUESTIONS

Explore the Falseness Within You and Beyond You to Get Rid of It

1. Is there a particular person you tend to lie to? Or perhaps there are certain situations where you find that you are more likely to become deceptive. Why is this?
2. Have you ever worked hard to convince someone else that something was true? When you did this, was it because you also had some doubts of your own?
3. What did you know to be true when you were 5, 10, 15, 20, 30, 40, 50, etc., years old, up to now? What has changed in time?
4. When people are too polite or too rigid about following social rules, does this feel false to you? Does it feel like they are genuinely polite people, or are they too worried about following the rules of politeness?
5. What kinds of false ideas are you being exposed to every day? Are they difficult to perceive consciously because you have seen them so often?

TAKE ACTION TODAY

Explore the Falseness Within You and
Beyond You to Get Rid of It

Action: **Spend some time quietly with yourself.** You can enter a meditative state if you have practice doing this, but if not, just sit quietly for several minutes. Focus on your breathing, and allow yourself to reach a calm and peaceful state.

Then, imagine yourself, but an older, wiser version. Perhaps you can imagine yourself, but twenty or thirty years older.

Ask your older self:

What is the biggest falsehood that I have allowed into my life, and how can I overcome this?

What is the greatest truth in my life, which I should work to maintain and grow?

You may ask yourself any other questions on your mind and perhaps questions about your life direction, purpose, or how to overcome a particular obstacle.

Reason: Who knows you better than yourself? Remember that you are the only one who will be able to figure out your truth. No one can give it to you. So it makes sense to ask for help from another version of yourself. As strange of an idea as this may seem, give it a chance. You may surprise yourself.

Tip: If you struggle with this exercise, do not try to force it. You can always try again at another time. When you first try this exercise, you may not realize how profound the wisdom is that you receive. I recommend writing down any insights you gain from conversations with yourself.

The Liar's Scale (Some Lies Are Worse Than Others)

> "Those who have failed to work toward the truth have missed the purpose of living."
>
> — Buddha

Note: this section was originally posted on my site: www.RobledoThoughts. com. On your journey to exploring the falseness within you, I believe it will help to examine the types of lies you tell or lies that people around you tend to tell. In seeing the lies for what they are, we can redirect ourselves back toward truth.

All lies are not the same, so I want you to consider how some lies can be worse than others.

On the path to seeking Truth in our lives, we need to think about this. Suppose we don't consciously focus on how truthful we are or how honest the people or systems around us are. In that case, our lives can descend into falseness. We may tell bigger and bigger lies and become surrounded by falseness. Then one day, truth and falseness can blur together.

We should always maintain our grasp on truth because doing so means grasping reality. To help you maintain a better hold on truth and reality,

I present you with **The Liar's Scale.** Keep in mind that lower numbers indicate lesser lies, and larger numbers are for bigger lies.

1) The Survivor's Lie

The purpose of these lies is to meet personal needs—such as food, water, shelter, or other necessary comforts. When telling such lies, the primary goal is to survive, not take more than necessary.

2) The Positive Lie (E.g., "White Lie")

The purpose of this lie is not to cause any harm and not to hide any misdeeds. The aim is usually to help prevent someone from feeling bad, or to help someone feel better. Your goal is to somehow improve the situation for someone else by telling a positive lie.

3) The Minor Lie

These are small lies that we may tell to get our way in trivial situations. The purpose may be to help others in some way. Still, we are often more interested in helping ourselves feel better or avoid a negative consequence rather than on how this lie impacts others.

4) The "Saving Face" Lie

This is a lie where you make up an excuse or state something just to avoid looking bad. At this stage, you want to manage how people think of you, even if this involves lying to them. Rather than being motivated to make people think you are the best, you don't want them to think less of you. With the "Saving Face" lie, you lie about who you are, which seems more significant than the prior lies on the scale.

5) The "I Can't Fail" Lie

With this type of lie, you had a goal in your life, and you have realized that you could not meet it normally. To complete it then, you have decided to either tell a lie or to cheat in some way to get your desired outcome. At this stage, the lie should only be an isolated or rare incident and not a regular occurrence. However, this type of lie is higher than the prior ones because to avoid derailing your entire life or losing a job, people can be motivated to tell much bigger lies (or to cheat in substantial ways).

6) The "I Must Win" Lie

Here, the need to always win or be right or better than others will result in lying to keep a competitive edge and maintain the illusion of being the best. You are determined to be highly competitive or possibly the best, even if it means telling big lies. This is a larger lie than the prior ones because you have decided on an outcome you must meet. You will do anything to get that outcome, which includes lying or cheating to meet that objective.

7) The "I Will Protect You" Lie

With this type of lie, someone is aware of an improper action (by themselves or someone else). This person lies (or purposely does not state the truth) to protect someone from learning about this bad action. Someone may tell themselves that they lie to protect others. Still, they are often lying to protect themselves from the backlash they will receive if others learn the truth. This lie is high on the scale because these lies can quickly turn into more lies to cover up prior lies. It is also high on the list because, generally speaking, this involves lies that people consider to be major breaches of trust or integrity. Otherwise, they would not expend so much energy in maintaining this type of lie.

8) The "I Will Hurt You" Lie

The above lies are usually not intended to cause harm, which is why this lie is higher up on the scale. At this point, a person is motivated to harm others—it may be to "teach them a lesson" or because someone has personal reasons for disliking another person. Such lies may be used to acquire money or valuables or to cause psychological or physical harm.

9) The "My Life is a Lie" Lie

At this stage, someone has discovered that lying is a powerful tool for getting what they want. With this type of lie, a person may gain sympathy by making things up or exaggerating his problems to absurd degrees. He may make up stories to entice people to give him money. Whenever his integrity or expertise is called into question, he may have lies ready to support his behavior. At this stage, significant aspects of a person's life may have been fabricated. The resume may be mostly made up of falsehoods, and his attire may make it seem as if he is much more successful than he is. Relationships may be based on promises that he never intended to follow through on. At this level, a person is so used to lying that when they are inevitably caught in a lie, they make up new "facts" to support a made-up story that justifies their actions.

The "Keeping the Justice" Lie

Another type of lie that will not be easily ranked above is the **"Keeping the Justice" Lie**, where someone lies to uphold some greater sense of justice or values. This one will be kept unranked because, in the end, we must all make our judgment calls as to whether it is worth it to try to keep the justice or not. And we may all have different impressions of what is justified.

I'm interested in discussing lies because it happens quite a lot, and we tend to accept it as a way of life. Anything someone tells you or anything that you read today may be a lie. We are all aware of this and probably have made some level of peace with this.

Unfortunately, the more lies a person tells, the more likely they are to fall into a pattern of telling deeper and bigger lies. At the highest stages of lying, a person's life consists more of lies than truth. When they get up in the morning, the first thing that runs through their minds is which made-up stories they have to tell which individuals to get the desired results. Otherwise, they will focus on protecting all of their prior lies from being discovered.

Even at lower stages of lying, you can easily slip into deeper levels. Imagine if someone perpetually tells minor lies (#3 on the scale). These may be small lies, but in time this person may slip deeper and deeper down the scale as lying becomes a regular part of their life.

I would encourage you to become more conscious of any lies you may tell in your life. Sometimes, they can become so routine that we fail even to notice them. For example, perhaps there is someone in your life who lies to you regularly. If you "go along" with these lies, then in a sense, you are lying too.

If someone lies to you or those around you often, think about what you can do to break this cycle where they "sell" you their lies, and you appear to "buy" into them. We should find ways to reduce the lying around us because people who do this regularly may not even be conscious of what they are doing. And if they think they are getting away with it, they may be motivated to continue. Perhaps this is a bad habit they developed, and they will not stop unless they are called out on it somehow.

Here are some remarks I have made in the past or that I might make if I hear something that is an apparent lie:

- "Really? That's not what someone else told me."
- "Where are you getting your facts from? I don't think I would trust that source."

- "Some people are concerned with [insert whatever sense of integrity or value the person is aiming to protect with this lie], but I couldn't care less."
- "So what do you think about [mention another topic]?" Or "Look at the time—I have to get going." (This can get them to see that you will not sit by and listen to lies.)
- "Wow, that is truly unbelievable—that is one for the record books (said with slight sarcasm)."
- "Now you are just making stuff up (not in an irritated tone, but possibly a slightly amused tone)."
- "I wasn't born yesterday, you know."
- "Now that just flies in the face of everything I know to be true (I may save this one for a pathological liar)."

Think back to times you have noticed that someone was most likely lying. If you pay attention, you can often spot signals that will indicate someone *may* be lying. For example:

- There is an inconsistency in what someone has stated. Perhaps they often claim to be whatever is advantageous at the moment, which may result in conflicting statements.
- Their body language or tone of voice is out of sync with the words they use. For example, they may tell you bad news in a happy tone of voice.
- They always have excuses to avoid having to do undesirable activities.
- They tend to get overly defensive, and their tone of voice rises sharply.
- They become uncomfortable and touch their nose or face as they speak.
- They closely monitor your reaction, possibly to see if you are "buying" their story. They may check for your response to judge if they should continue with their story or modify it to appease you.
- They make claims that do not have common sense or reason behind them—and they do this regularly.

KEY QUESTIONS

The Liar's Scale

1. What types of lies do you tend to tell?
2. On average, where do they fall on the Liar's Scale?
3. Have your lies gotten smaller or bigger in time?
4. What about the people around you. How much do you think they lie, and are you doing anything about it?
5. Are you harder on others when they lie or harder on yourself when you lie? Do you have a double standard?

TAKE ACTION TODAY

The Liar's Scale

Action: **Today, put in the extra work to be as truthful as you can be about *everything*.** Even if you are going through negative emotions, such as anxiety or confusion, consider sharing this with someone. If you make a mistake, be direct about what happened, rather than making excuses or denying your role.

This isn't to imply that you would normally lie, but pay close attention to your instincts. In some situations, we may become naturally defensive and feel that it is okay to say anything necessary to defend our position. Of course, such an approach can result in lies.

When you focus on consciously telling the truth today, keep in mind how this makes you feel. Do you feel better about yourself and like you are more True to yourself because you have represented yourself as truthfully as possible?

Reason: It is generally best to tell the truth. When we lie about something, we will always worry that someone may discover this lie and that we could get punished for it in the future. When you tell the truth, you do not need to worry. Also, in telling the truth, you will be more likely to attract people in your life who believe the truth is important and value you as you are. If you make a mistake, those who appreciate the truth will understand that you are human and not expect perfection. They will be willing to give you another chance just because you told the truth.

Tip: There are different degrees of truth. I tend to get a feeling when I know that I am hiding something that people around me deserve to know about. When you get that feeling, take it seriously. If you're uncomfortable telling everyone your truth, consider taking a close friend or perhaps your boss or someone you trust and explaining your truth to them.

Test Your Truth

"Do not flinch from experiences that might destroy your beliefs. The thought you cannot think controls you more than thoughts you speak aloud. Submit yourself to ordeals and test yourself in fire. Relinquish the emotion which rests upon a mistaken belief, and seek to feel fully that emotion which fits the facts."

— Eliezer Yudkowsky

What do you do when you think you have your truth? Does this mean you have arrived at your destination? Not exactly.

As I've said before, Truth is a journey.

This book has not been about arriving anywhere. There may be no destination to arrive at.

In my experience, most of us do not want anyone to test us, to *truly test us*. We want to have our beliefs or our truths and to be content with this. We don't want to be challenged—we feel safer to continue believing in our truths, even if they are not entirely true.

When someone pokes holes in your truth, it feels like they are poking holes in your spirit. Nonetheless, we need to learn to deal with criticisms and flaws. No one is perfect, after all. This may open us up to hurtful comments, but we will be stronger for it in the end.

I would urge that you not find a particular "truth" and then stick to it stubbornly for all of eternity. Be willing to test it, reevaluate it, and reconsider it. Has something changed? Is there new information that is worth considering?

Imagine this: Martin is a fish in the ocean who knows nothing but wetness. To Martin, everything is wet, and so he cannot fully perceive the idea of what it means to be wet. To know what it means to be wet, he would have to know what it means to be dry, right? Then one day, a fisherman hooks Martin, and he finds himself in a boat. The hot sun is quickly drying him up. For the first time, he sees that not all is wet. Now he sees the truth, that it is possible to become dry by leaving the ocean.

In this story, I am the fisherman.

And I decide that Martin should get to experience wetness once again so that he can learn to appreciate his life more fully. I choose to toss him back in the ocean. (Splash!)

Martin could never consciously test his truth that everything was wet because for him, to leave the ocean is to die. But as humans, we can test our truths. Testing them will not kill us, even if it may feel unpleasant. We have to be willing to be uncomfortable and conduct these tests to figure out the whole truth of our lives. Alternatively, we can assume that we know all the facts and become upset when other people disagree. That is not ideal.

There are two key ways to test your truth. **The first way to test your truth is to allow yourself to assume that you may be wrong, and to look for alternative and better options.** This simple approach will force you to behave differently. It will enable you to perhaps discover a new truth that had remained hidden from you.

Consider that perhaps your truth is that a co-worker named Noah is mean to you and that he does not like you. Because you usually assume this to be the case, you tend to be in a bad mood around him. Then, perhaps your bad mood puts Noah in a bad mood too, and this just reaffirms your truth, that Noah does not like you. A way to test this truth isn't to do the same thing you always do. Instead, you can test it by ensuring you are in a good mood before seeing Noah and being nice to him. If you are nice to Noah, does he still react negatively? The only way to know is to test this truth for yourself.

In another scenario, perhaps your truth is that you are not good at math. Then, whenever there is math to be done, you always get a friend or family member to do it for you. Whenever you try to do some math on your own, you are often wrong, and so you get used to the idea that you are simply not any good at math. The way to test this would be actually to commit yourself to improve your math skills. It would mean no longer asking for help on simple math problems, instead taking the time to practice and improve. Perhaps, you could even take a class or get a tutor to help improve.

As a final scenario, let's consider emotions or moods. What if you just got into a major fight with your significant other, and you feel terrible about it. You may even think the worst. You could start thinking that you are tired of this relationship and all you want to do is get away from it. It may cross your mind that it is time for you to end it, or you may wonder if this time your significant other will get fed up and want to end it. Then, perhaps you get sad, or angry, or upset in some way. Of course, these are not fun thoughts to have. When this happens, you can ask if these thoughts reflect the truth, or if you are just upset, and if this is something that will pass. The point here is sometimes to take a step back and assume that your thoughts could be wrong. Instead of assuming that you are headed for a breakup, you may recall that you usually work out your problems, so surely you will fix them again this time.

As I said, there are two main ways to test your truth. The first way was to assume that your truth may be wrong. This can be productive when you have a "truth" that is not working out well.

The second way to test your truth is to assume that you are right and push yourself to live by that truth more fully. This is a more helpful way to test your truths when you have a deeper part of yourself, such as a core value you choose to live your life by.

If your truth is kindness, then test it. Try being kind to those who do you wrong. Be kind to someone who you do not know well. Be kind even when you are having a bad day.

If your truth is gratitude, then test it. Be grateful first thing in the morning and the last thing at night before bedtime. Be thankful for the hard lessons learned as well as the goodness bestowed upon you. Appreciate the duties people in your life perform, even when they are paid for them.

If your truth is intelligence, then test it. See and judge yourself as if you saw yourself from afar. Evaluate your words, thoughts, and actions and see if they are logical and congruent. Learn and read every day. Challenge your mind to see, think, and calculate more deeply than you ever have, even when this is boring and difficult.

If your truth is empathy, then test it. See a tired older woman at a bus stop, and ask yourself what her day was like. Did she struggle, work hard, suffer, doubt, or make progress? See a teenager skateboarding in ripped jeans, and ask yourself what his life is like. Does he have a stable home, get good grades, have close friends, and will he become somebody important? See a homeless person sleeping outside in the cold, and ask yourself how he is doing. Is he sick, lonely, tired, or hungry? Does he have anyone in the world who cares about him? Then, can you extend your empathy beyond thought and feel what they feel? Can you find it in yourself to take helpful actions based on that empathy? Are you able to extend your compassion to others even when you are tired and worn down yourself?

If your truth is responsibility, then test it. When you promised to help too many people, will you do your best to live up to those promises, even when it means working harder and sleeping less? When you are in charge of a task, and the situation becomes daunting, will you rise to the occasion and make sure everything is taken care of?

If your truth is independence, then test it. Instead of asking people for help all of the time, first look for ways to resolve problems on your own. Only ask for help when you need it when you cannot make progress on your own.

Consider this scenario: What if Lucas just got out of prison? He spent years there, and now he is ready to redeem himself. He's eager to find a steady job, but as he applies everywhere that he can, a pattern emerges. When the employer finds out that he has spent time in prison, they lose interest in hiring him. Lucas recalls that he still knows where old contacts live that could help get him a "job," no questions asked. The problem is that if he falls into those old patterns, he will surely end up behind bars soon enough. Instead, Lucas decides that his truth is being tested here. In this case, his truth is his discipline and his commitment to living righteously, even when it is the hard path. He decides that even if he has to move to get a job, he will do it. Even if he has to work for less pay, he'll do it. He is willing to be tested and let his truth shine through in the end.

Truth is a powerful word. Take a moment to ask yourself if you are living a truthful life. To me, truth means consistency. We cannot expect perfection. Just because you value happiness does not mean that you can never be sad. That would be unrealistic. But if you value happiness, are you taking daily actions that move you in that direction? Are you doing this consistently, choosing joy over sadness at every opportunity, or are you just making excuses?

Every day we are tested. But we fail to understand that this is the case. We think—just this one time, I will be lazy. Just this one time, I will abandon my values and take the easy road. Just this one time, I can act impulsively and forget about what matters. Just this one time, I can prioritize what makes me feel good now, even when that interferes with my values.

We have to learn that every day and every moment is a test—and we can decide to move toward the path of our truth or walk away from it. The choice is yours.

Often, we become our own biggest obstacles. We either create our obstacles or allow others to put them on our path. Then we do not adequately confront them according to our values. Understand that the barriers are not the problem. By being presented with them, you have an opportunity to practice your values more deeply and find your truth.

But you must train every day. You must live by your values every day. Test your truths and test them regularly. When the big moment happens, and you face the most difficult decisions and situations of your life, you will be ready for it.

Every day is a test. Every day is helping you to train toward becoming something. Sometimes, the universe provides us with many challenging tests. But other times, it gives us a break. When the universe is not thoroughly testing you, you should consider testing your deepest truths for yourself.

Test Your Truth

1. What is a truth that is not working out so well for you, where you could benefit from testing it and assuming it could be wrong?
2. What is a truth that is a part of you, such as a core value? Can you push yourself to live by this truth more fully?
3. Is there some truth in the opposite of what you think to be true?
4. Think of a particular truth in your life that you have some doubt about—could it be worth testing?
5. What was the last time one of your deeply held truths was tested? What did you learn?

TAKE ACTION TODAY

Test Your Truth

Action: What is a truth in your life that you have just assumed to be true for the longest time? Think of different beliefs you may have. **How would you fill in these blanks?**

For the most part, people are: _____

Everyone was born with the right to: _____

No matter how tempting, no one should ever: _____

The most important thing in life is: _____

Use your answers to these statements to figure out a truth in your life that you may not have tested properly. For any answers you give to key questions in your life, ask if you have considered alternatives. Is your way of seeing things necessarily the absolute truth? Is there another option or perspective that is also worth considering?

Today, for one of your core truths, look up information or evidence that *may* disconfirm that truth. Look up reasons why it may be false or misguided. Then, instead of resisting that information, attempt to open your mind to it.

Reason: Many of us go through life just assuming that we have the truth and the answers. Our truths seem so obvious to us that we fail to consider alternative perspectives or truths. We become blinded and see things through one narrow viewpoint. For this reason, we should test our truths, to challenge ourselves, and encourage learning and personal growth.

Tip: The way to test your truth isn't to do the same things in the same ways as always. It may help to experiment and try behaving in one way for some cases and in another way for other situations. For example, suppose you enjoy telling jokes and think that this helps you make friends more easily. In that case, you can test that truth by telling jokes at some gatherings and not at other gatherings. It makes sense that your jokes can make people like you, but how would you truly know unless you tested this? Test more and more of your truths, more and more deeply. You will find that some of your "truths" were not entirely True.

Final Thoughts

"Believe me: It is no teaching and no instruction
that I give you. On what basis should I presume
to teach you? I give you news of the way of
this man, but not of your own way. My path is
not your path, therefore I cannot teach you.
Within us is the way, the truth, and the life."

— Carl Jung, *The Red Book* (Liber Novus)

Following your truth is not always going to be easy. I have lost mine and found it again many times. What is important is that you pay attention to the signs your mind and body give you. If you are perpetually annoyed, unhappy, or stressed, then you may have wandered away from your truth.

The truth can be ugly at times, but by shining a light on it, we will be more likely to find our way to a path that is true to ourselves, which is ultimately for the greater good. If we ignore the truth, we will just become wanderers, lost, and in need of direction.

I am curious: in the chapter, *Identify Your Values to Use as an Inner Compass That Illuminates Your True Path*, was Truth one of your highest values? For me, it is. I realized long ago that the truth could lead me to inconvenient places. The truth doesn't care about our feelings, desires, or wants. The truth isn't there to make us feel good or help us with a particular goal.

The truth just is.

When I was 16 years old, I decided that Truth was my highest value. Even if I learned or discovered things that I did not want to believe, I would let the truth guide me. I wanted to operate in the world of what is, not just in the world of what I wanted to be. They are not completely in contradiction. If you know the truth as it is, you can use that knowledge to create a life or environment that you desire.

I recommend finding someone you trust, with whom you can be open about your deepest truths. If you are willing to be brave, you may even spread your truth further. For example, you may discuss it among friends or blog about it. In having your truths out in the open, you will be allowing others to find any possible mistakes in your assumptions, reasoning, or ideas. You may even set yourself up to be rejected by people who disagree with you. And this could make you feel vulnerable, but it can ultimately be empowering. The choice is yours as to how open you wish to be with your truths. Still, if we share them and are available to each other's points of view, we will grow spiritually. We will learn more about ourselves, the people around us, and the world itself.

As a brief example of what it means to be open with our truth, I would like to tell you a short story. A family friend left a deep impression on me long ago. Ana always seemed outgoing and optimistic, and I had never noticed any particular issues with her. But one day, she mentioned some of her problems to my family and me. She was diagnosed with depression and anxiety disorders and was taking medication and seeing a therapist for this. She made me feel as if this were an everyday topic, and it was natural for her to tell us about it. And, of course, no one judged or criticized her for sharing this. We just listened and accepted her for who she was. She was our friend.

Yet I couldn't help but think—I would never have been so open about something like that. At that point in my life, many, many years ago, I simply would not discuss any mental health issues. I couldn't even imagine myself discussing something like that with a doctor, let alone my family or friends. I would have felt embarrassed and too self-conscious even to consider it.

Years later (or over a decade ago, as of this writing), I did fall into a deep depression, and I did keep it all to myself. This stubbornness only led me to fall further into depression. I neglected to get help until I was bedridden and had no other option. At that time, I remembered Ana's strength and courage, and I decided that it was time to speak my truth.

I called up friends, my parents, my brother, doctors, my boss, and colleagues. I told them what I was going through, and it released some of the power from the depression, and I started to become myself once again. After I opened this faucet of truth, it was hard to stop. I wanted people to understand why I had felt the need to keep my pains all to myself—but that didn't matter anymore. The truth had shone down on me—I had seen the light, and I was ready to speak about it.

Some people were understanding. Some felt hurt that I had not mentioned this to them sooner. Some seemed confused and unsure how they could help me—maybe they were surprised to see someone speak the truth so clearly. But I think everyone tried to help me and tried to understand in their way.

I have been following my truth for as long as I can remember. Sometimes, I felt that I failed at this, but somehow I was always led back to my authentic self.

Now, I would like to share the most difficult decision I ever made—it was one that I made because I valued my truth more than anything else.

At 25 years old (a decade ago), I was in my third year of a Ph.D. program, studying industrial-organizational psychology. I had thought about quitting many, many times, but I never did. I felt that continuing along was what I was supposed to do, even though most days I felt like an imposter in my own life. Day by day, I was losing interest in my work and in the direction my career was taking me. I had acquired a robotic level of efficiency by my third year. I was on top of all of my work, often finishing assignments and deadlines ahead of time.

Yet gradually, my whole life had become just a series of tasks that I needed to do. There wasn't anything more to my life. I had arranged my schedule to work from 8 am to 7 pm every day, except Sundays when I took a break. I executed this pattern like a machine. Life was just work that I had lost interest in, punctuated by short breaks. Eventually, my so-called reward would be to graduate to higher levels of responsibility and work, with less time off. That is what I had to "look forward to."

One day, something in my robotic efficiency had broken. I failed to perform my work adequately. I simply could not understand what I was expected to do on a particular task assigned to me. Or perhaps I was unable to communicate that I did not understand something. I had been getting by on little enthusiasm for so long and an empty-minded level of efficiency. Despite this, somehow, I held on to the belief that things would turn out okay. Eventually, I felt that I would be inspired and motivated. But this wasn't happening. And it seemed in my lack of motivation and lack of understanding that I had committed some significant mistakes on the task I was assigned to do. Ultimately, some of my colleagues had to redo my work the night before a deadline.

I had become overconfident, thinking that I would keep making progress, but there were kinks in my system. I wasn't concerned with how the work went. Instead, I just wanted to keep up the appearances that I was getting my job done correctly. Of course, to keep up the impressions that I was doing my work, I needed to do it correctly. This time, I had failed in that respect.

Rather than dealing with my mistake, I ended up taking a thirteen-hour car ride to visit my family. On that ride, I realized what I had to do. I needed to leave it all behind. I had gotten my B.A. in psychology, and I had recently received my M.S. in industrial-organizational psychology. It was clear to me that continuing on this path toward the Ph.D. was not in me. It was not my truth. This path was not leading me toward myself but away from myself. I was becoming more and more distant, hardly recognizing myself or what I had become.

When my colleagues saw me, I had a sick feeling inside that they were not seeing me. That they could not see me because my role as a Ph.D. student had become my identity. My true self had ceased to matter, and I was just a machine on autopilot, being productive until I had "broken" and failed to work properly. In the end, my failure to complete a project was just a nuisance for some of my colleagues. My boss was never even informed about it. I was under no threat of being punished, much less being kicked out of the program.

Nonetheless, I made my choice. It was my time to go.

The most difficult choice of my life was to follow my truth in this case. The program I was in had an unusually high track record for graduating students to the Ph.D. level, at around 95%. This made it extra difficult to be the one person who decided to leave.

I wasn't sure which direction my life would go in from there. There was no firm ground to land on. No plan. I had simply realized that this path was too far away from my truth, and I needed to find a new one. I didn't want to wake up at 50 years old, realizing that my whole life's path had been just a lie.

Despite having no idea what life had in store for me, I abandoned the path that was leading me toward falseness. And I proceeded toward truth. Going on that path has led me to write this book, *Your Personal Truth*.

The truth is the way to go. It helps you to see more clearly and gives less power to whatever is bothering you. When I reveal my truth to family and loved ones, this helps me clarify the direction that I need to go in. Your family and loved ones should want to help you live your truth and help you move in that direction. If you don't tell them your truth to begin with, how can they ever help you?

If it seems like a great leap to share your truths with others, start sharing them with yourself. Meditate and think about them deeply. Write them down in a journal. Share them with a therapist or life coach if you would like. Start somewhere, but don't just bury your truths deep inside and forget about them.

Searching for your truth is not always easy. I make mistakes like anyone else. I have been led astray at times. I have forgotten to follow my inner compass of values at some points. But this is the journey. The road away from truth just leads you back to it anyway. You can only run so far away from it before it pulls you back in.

In the end, all will be okay.

Open your mind to the truth, yet understand that the more you open your mind, the more you will be in a vulnerable position and potentially allow falseness to enter. This is why you must always test your truths. Do not allow any random thought to fly into your mind as a wrench into a machine, throwing you off balance. Test your truths before you adopt them as your own and incorporate them into your being. And when you have them, continue to test them to make sure that they are your personal truths.

Open-mindedness is an excellent quality to have, but it must be combined with critical thinking and testing to help you arrive at deeper truths. In its simplest form, *open-mindedness* is being willing to consider that another perspective could have merit. And *critical thinking* is being willing to question something rather than assuming that it is entirely accurate. *Testing* is taking action to confirm or disconfirm whether what you think is true is reflected by reality. Use all of these tools to help you arrive at something closer to the truth.

All we can do is learn about ourselves and the universe, discover our truths, move away from the falseness, and test our truths. Then, as we find more accurate truths, we can release ourselves from the old ones that were not quite right for us.

If we keep doing this, at some point, our personal truth and the universal truth will become one.

My parting words to you: I hope you find the courage to be true to yourself and to spread some of that truth to others. Then, when others conflict with your personal truth, I hope you can see that they have a part of the truth as well. Some ideas may be worth fighting for when necessary, but when not truly necessary, we should learn to see that we can all have our truths, and live our truths, and let others have theirs, and live theirs as well.

I have shared my truth with you and aspired to share a universal truth as well. You should now be one step closer to Your Personal Truth.

KEY QUESTIONS

Final Thoughts

1. What is the most profound truth that you have ever revealed to someone? What happened as a result?
2. What is the deepest truth that someone ever revealed to you? What did you think, or how did you react?
3. Have you ever told the truth, and people did not believe you or did not react in the way you expected?
4. Are the truths in your life helping or hurting you? Would it benefit you to reconsider your personal truths?
5. Has your perspective on truth changed as a result of reading *Your Personal Truth*? In what way?

TAKE ACTION TODAY

Final Thoughts

Action: **Think of a deep truth hidden within.** It may be something you saw or something that you did. Is there a truth you've been hiding within you, afraid to let out? This may be a feeling or emotion, a painful situation you are coping with, or something you regret having done.

When you have this truth in mind that perhaps has been weighing you down, or disrupting your life somehow, consider doing the unthinkable. **Share that truth with someone.**

If you are worried about sharing your truth, you may start with a confidential source. For example, you could share it with a priest or a trusted person in your religion, a psychologist, or a close friend or family member.

You may decide that it's time to stop hiding a particular truth from the world. Perhaps there is something about yourself that you were worried that people would find out. Instead of hiding this anymore, you may simply stop keeping that a secret. If you are not ready, then do not share it openly—yet, consider not hiding it either.

Reason: This is like a final exam, now that you have finished the book. Take a deep truth, and be willing to reveal it and discuss it. As difficult and painful as this may be, it will help you learn more deeply about yourself and be sure that you have learned and transformed yourself. By being challenged, our truths can grow and become more firm. But if we ignore them and deny them, we may fail to meet our full potential.

Tip: If you are not ready to reveal this truth to anyone else or are concerned that it could do more harm, then it can be helpful to reflect on it for yourself. What does this truth mean to you now if it is still on your mind? Have you grown from it? Or in having tried to hide it, have you obstructed your growth somehow?

Consider journaling your truth. Of course, if you do not want anyone to discover this, then be sure to secure your journal. A journal can be a form of sharing your truth with yourself. I have written my truths in a journal in the past, and it can be a therapeutic experience. It can give you a sense of relief as if you've shared it. This is because you will be more likely to explore your feelings, thoughts, and truths more deeply through writing than you would have otherwise.

Thank You

Thank you for taking the time to read *Your Personal Truth*. I hope that you found the information useful. Just remember that a key part of the learning process is putting what you read into practice.

Before you go, I want to invite you to pick up three *free gifts*:

1. **Searching for Truth**—an exclusive eBook that is not available to the public.
2. A list of **I. C. Robledo's Top Book Recommendations**—a resource that is updated regularly.
3. **Step Up Your Learning**: Free Tools to Learn Almost Anything—a free guide.

All you have to do is type this into your web browser:

Mentalmax.net/EN

Also, if you have any questions, comments, or feedback about this book, you can send me a message, and I'll get back to you as soon as possible. My email address is:

ic.robledo@mentalmax.net

I. C. Robledo's Thoughts

I am in charge of a project designed to help us all **pursue higher states of Consciousness, Understanding, and Being.**

This is a website where I share my deepest Truths.

If you have enjoyed this book, I would be honored if you would read some Thoughts from my website. Below are some posts you may find particularly interesting:

- Find Your Inner Truth
- The Forces that Pull Us Apart and Make Us Who We Are
- The Path to a True and Fruitful Life
- Think of Death to Live More Consciously
- Approaching Higher Levels of Consciousness
- Be More, Do Less
- The Paradox of the Model Citizen
- What Are You Training Mentally for?
- Who Can Truly Teach You?

This is a project of love for me, where all I want to do is spread my best Thoughts into the world to help you *live your best life.*

You can read all of my Thoughts *for free* here: www.RobledoThoughts.com

Did You Learn Something New?

If you found this book useful, insightful, or valuable, please consider writing a review online. Your input makes a big difference, as it will help readers like you to decide whether to check out this book next.

More Books by I. C. Robledo

The Intellectual Toolkit of Geniuses
Master Your Focus
The Smart Habit Guide
No One Ever Taught Me How to Learn
Ready, Set, Change
The Secret Principles of Genius
Idea Hacks
Practical Memory
365 Quotes to Live Your Life By
7 Thoughts to Live Your Life By
The Insightful Reader
Question Yourself

To stay up to date with I. C. Robledo's new books, please visit Robledothoughts.com/books or sign up to receive updates at Mentalmax. net/EN.

Printed in Great Britain
by Amazon